KU-241-164

TOP
100

QUICK MEALS

TOP
100
QUICK MEALS

SAFEWAY/GOOD HOUSEKEEPING

Text and illustrations copyright © Ebury Press and the
National Magazine Company Ltd 1993

All rights reserved. No part of this publication may be
reproduced in any form or by any means without permission.

Published exclusively for
Safeway
6 Millington Road, Hayes, Middlesex UB3 4AY
by Ebury Press
A division of Random House
20 Vauxhall Bridge Road
London SW1V 2SA

First published 1993

Edited by Felicity Jackson and Beverly Le Blanc
Designed by Peartree Design Associates
'Special photography by Ken Field
Food stylist Kerenza Harries
Photographic stylists Sue Russell and Suzy Gittins

The paper in this book is acid-free

Typeset by Textype Typesetters, Cambridge
Printed in Italy

ISBN 0 09 182100 2

COOKERY NOTES

All spoon measures are level unless otherwise stated.

Size 2 eggs should be used except when otherwise stated.

Granulated sugar is used unless otherwise stated.

The oven should be preheated to the required
temperature unless otherwise stated.

Contents

MEAL-IN-ONE SOUPS
— 8 —

SUBSTANTIAL SALADS
— 16 —

PIZZAS, PASTA AND RICE
— 26 —

GRATINS AND QUICK BAKES
— 38 —

DELICIOUS GRILLS
— 46 —

STIR-FRIES AND SAUTÉS
— 54 —

INSTANT DESSERTS
— 68 —

INDEX
— 80 —

FOREWORD

TOP 100 QUICK MEALS is one of a popular new series of colourful and practical cookery books created for Safeway customers. It contains 100 *Good Housekeeping* recipes, each one quick to prepare and delicious to eat.

The Good Housekeeping Institute is unique in the field of food and cookery, and every recipe has been created and double-tested in the Institute's world-famous kitchens.

There are recipes to suit all occasions, from meal-in-one soups and substantial salads to quick bakes and gratins. For those with a sweet tooth there is a mouthwatering selection of instant desserts.

Helpful cook's tips give you time-saving advice, making this an invaluable book for those who love cooking but are short of time.

COOKERY EDITOR
GOOD HOUSEKEEPING

HADDOCK AND CORN CHOWDER

SERVES 4-6

25-50 g (1-2 oz) butter or margarine
450 g (1 lb) old potatoes, peeled and diced
225 g (8 oz) onion, skinned and thinly sliced
½ × 5 ml tsp chilli powder
600 ml (20 fl oz) vegetable stock
600 ml (20 fl oz) milk
salt and pepper
225 g (8 oz) fresh haddock fillet, skinned and
   broken into bite-sized pieces
225 g (8 oz), smoked haddock fillet, skinned and
   broken into bite-sized pieces
198 g can sweetcorn kernels
115 g (4 oz) cooked peeled prawns
chopped fresh parsley

1. Heat the butter in a large saucepan and fry
the vegetables and the chilli powder for 2-3
minutes until beginning to soften.
2. Pour in the stock and milk with a little
seasoning. Bring to the boil, then cover and
simmer for 10 minutes.
3. Add the haddock to the pan with the corn.
Return to the boil, then cover and simmer
until the potatoes are tender and the fish begins
to flake apart. Skim the surface as necessary.
4. Stir in the prawns with plenty of parsley.
Adjust seasoning and serve at once.

COOK'S TIP This hearty, old-fashioned
chowder is equally delicious made with other
fish. You can use cod or whiting, or fresh
salmon if you are feeling extravagant. For extra
colour, sauté a finely-diced red pepper with the
other vegetables.

Haddock and Corn Chowder

CHUNKY LENTIL SOUP

SERVES 4-6

225 g (8 oz) split red lentils
2 × 15 ml tbs oil
50 g (2 oz) onion, skinned and thinly sliced
115 g (4 oz) carrot, peeled and thinly sliced
75 g (3 oz) celery, thinly sliced
1.8 lt (3 pt) chicken or vegetable stock
227 g can chopped tomatoes
1 garlic clove, skinned and crushed
½ × 5 ml tsp chilli powder
salt and pepper

1. Place the lentils in a sieve and rinse well. Put in a pan of boiling water and boil rapidly for 10 minutes. Drain.
2. Heat the oil in a medium-sized saucepan and fry the vegetables for 2-3 minutes until beginning to soften.
3. Add the remaining ingredients and bring to the boil. Cover and simmer gently for 15-20 minutes, or until all the ingredients are tender.

FRENCH BEAN SOUP

SERVES 4-6

2 × 15 ml tbs oil
115 g (4 oz) onion, skinned and finely chopped
450 g (1 lb) frozen French green beans
2 × 15 ml tbs plain flour
1 × 15 ml tbs chopped fresh parsley
900 ml (30 fl oz) chicken stock
150 ml (5 fl oz) milk
3 × 15 ml tbs soured cream or natural yogurt
    (optional)
salt and pepper
snipped grilled bacon or garlic croûtons, to garnish

1. Heat the oil in a large saucepan and fry the onion for 3-4 minutes until soft but not brown. Mix in the beans, flour, parsley and stock.

2. Bring to the boil, then cover and simmer for 10-12 minutes, stirring occasionally, or until the beans are quite tender.
3. Purée the soup in a blender or food processor. Return to the rinsed-out saucepan with the milk and reheat gently.
4. Stir in the soured cream or yogurt and adjust seasoning. Serve with snipped grilled bacon or garlic croûtons.

LENTIL AND COCONUT SOUP

SERVES 6

2 × 15 ml tbs olive oil
2 large garlic cloves, skinned and crushed
2.5 cm (1 in) piece fresh root ginger, peeled and
    finely chopped
6 × 15 ml tbs coconut-milk powder, or 50 g (2 oz)
    creamed coconut, chopped
3 × 15 ml tbs garlic and spring onion sauce
335 g (12 oz) red lentils, boiled rapidly for 10
    minutes then drained
425 ml (15 fl oz) chicken stock
3 × 15 ml tbs chopped fresh coriander
salt and pepper
natural yogurt and sprigs of fresh coriander,
    to garnish

1. Heat the oil in a large saucepan and fry the garlic and ginger until soft and golden.
2. Add all the remaining ingredients, except the coriander and garnish ingredients. Pour in 1.5 lt (2½ pt) water. Whisk vigorously, cover and simmer for about 15 minutes until the lentils are tender. Leave to cool slightly.
3. Blend the mixture with the chopped coriander in a food processor, then reheat gently, adjusting the seasoning to taste. Serve the soup garnished with natural yogurt and sprigs of fresh coriander.

Lentil and Coconut Soup

Purée of Broccoli with Stilton

SERVES 4

25 g (1 oz) butter or margarine
175 g (6 oz) onion, skinned and sliced
225 g (8 oz) broccoli, sliced
good pinch of cumin seeds
3 × 15 ml tbs red lentils, boiled rapidly for 10
   minutes then drained
900 ml (1½ pt) chicken stock
50 g (2 oz) Stilton cheese
salt and pepper
chopped fresh parsley, to garnish

1. Melt the butter in a large saucepan and fry the onion and broccoli with the cumin seeds for 2-3 minutes until starting to soften.
2. Stir in the lentils and chicken stock. Bring to the boil, then cover and simmer for about 15 minutes until all the ingredients are tender.
3. Purée the soup in a blender or food processor until smooth. Reheat, crumble in the Stilton and adjust seasoning. Garnish and serve.

White Bean and Basil Soup

SERVES 2-3

25 g (1 oz) butter or margarine
115 g (4 oz) onion, skinned and sliced
430 g can haricot beans, well drained and rinsed
1 vegetable stock cube
2-3 × 15 ml tbs pesto sauce
salt and pepper
chopped fresh parsley, to garnish

1. Melt the butter in a large saucepan and fry the onion for 2-3 minutes until softened. Add about two-thirds of the haricot beans, and the

vegetable stock cube dissolved in 600 ml (20 fl oz) hot water.
2. Bring to the boil, then cover and simmer for about 15 minutes.
3. Purée the soup in a blender or food processor. Return to the rinsed-out pan with the reserved beans and pesto.
4. Add seasoning to taste and simmer for a further 5 minutes. Serve garnished with parsley.

Spicy Bean and Courgette Soup

SERVES 4

2 × 15 ml tbs olive oil
175 g (6 oz) onion, skinned and finely chopped
2 garlic cloves, skinned and crushed
2 × 5 ml tsp ground coriander
1 × 15 ml tbs paprika
1 × 5 ml tsp mild curry powder
450 g (1 lb) courgettes, halved and sliced
225 g (8 oz) potatoes, peeled and diced
430 g can red kidney beans, drained and rinsed
400 g can flageolet beans, drained and rinsed
1.5 lt (2½ pt) vegetable stock
salt and pepper

1. Heat the oil in a saucepan and fry the onion and garlic for 2 minutes. Add the spices and cook, stirring, for 1 minute.
2. Mix in the courgettes and potatoes and cook for 1-2 minutes, stirring occasionally.
3. Add remaining ingredients, cover and simmer for 25 minutes, stirring occasionally, or until the potatoes are tender. Adjust seasoning before serving.

Spicy Bean and Courgette Soup

TOMATO SOUP WITH BACON

SERVES 2-3

2 × 15 ml tbs oil
115 g (4 oz) onion, skinned and thinly sliced
75 g (3 oz) lean bacon, rind removed and diced
430 g can butter beans, drained and rinsed
300 ml (10 fl oz) tomato juice
300 ml (10 fl oz) beef stock
1 × 5 ml tsp tomato purée
1 bay leaf
salt and pepper

1. Heat the oil in a medium-sized saucepan and fry the onion for 2-3 minutes until softened.
2. Add the bacon and cook for a further 2-3 minutes until it begins to brown, stirring frequently.
3. Add the beans and the remaining ingredients. Bring to the boil, then cover and simmer for about 15 minutes.
4. Remove the bay leaf and adjust seasoning before serving.

CHEESY VEGETABLE SOUP

SERVES 3-4

2 × 15 ml tbs oil
50 g (2 oz) onion, skinned and finely chopped
225 g (8 oz) old potatoes, peeled and diced
115 g (4 oz) courgettes, halved and thinly sliced
198 g can sweetcorn kernels, well drained
2 × 15 ml tbs plain flour
600 ml (20 fl oz) chicken stock
150 ml (5 fl oz) milk
large pinch of cayenne pepper (optional)
salt and pepper
150 g (5 oz) mature Cheddar cheese, grated

1. Heat the oil in a large saucepan and fry the onion for 3-4 minutes until soft but not brown.
2. Add the potatoes, courgettes and sweetcorn and fry until coated in oil. Stir in the flour and cook gently for 1-2 minutes, stirring. Add the stock with the milk, cayenne pepper and salt and pepper.
3. Bring to the boil, then cover and simmer gently for 10-12 minutes, or until the vegetables are tender. Stir in the cheese and adjust seasoning before serving.

ASPARAGUS SOUP

SERVES 4

115 g (4 oz) blanched almonds
1.2 lt (2 pt) vegetable stock or water
1 × 15 ml tbs vegetable oil
4 celery sticks, diced
450 g (1 lb) asparagus, trimmed and chopped
2 × 15 ml tbs chopped fresh parsley
3 × 15 ml tbs single cream
salt and pepper
cream, toasted flaked almonds and parsley, to
  garnish

1. Place the almonds and stock in a blender or food processor and grind until very smooth. Sieve the mixture, reserving the liquid, and discard the grains.
2. Heat the oil in a large pan and gently fry the celery for 5-6 minutes. Add the asparagus and cook for 5 minutes. Pour the stock over the top and add the parsley. Cover and simmer for 15 minutes.
3. Cool slightly, then purée in a blender or food processor until smooth. Return to the pan and stir in the cream. Heat gently. Season and garnish with cream, toasted almonds and parsley.

Asparagus Soup

AVOCADO AND CHICK-PEA SALAD

SERVES 4

3 × 15 ml tbs lemon juice
50 g (2 oz) fromage frais
115 ml (4 fl oz) milk
2 × 15 ml tbs chopped fresh chives or parsley
salt and pepper
1 avocado
450 g (1 lb) fresh young spinach, stalks removed
  and finely shredded
115 g (4 oz) radicchio lettuce, finely shredded
430 g can chick-peas, drained and rinsed
1 slice of wholemeal bread, toasted and cubed
2 eggs, hard-boiled and chopped
paprika

1. To make the dressing, place 2 × 15 ml tbs of the lemon juice, the fromage frais and milk in a bowl and whisk until smooth. Add the herbs and salt and pepper to taste. Set aside.
2. Peel the avocado, discard the stone and dice. Coat with the remaining lemon juice to prevent discoloration.
3. Mix together the spinach and radicchio leaves and arrange on a large serving platter. Scatter the avocado, chick-peas, toast cubes and eggs on top and sprinkle over a little paprika.
4. To serve, spoon a little of the dressing over the salad. Serve the remaining dressing separately.

VARIATION When preparing the dressing, reserve a few herbs to use as a garnish.

Avocado and Chick-Pea Salad (left)
Grilled Chicory and Asparagus Salad (right)

17

GRILLED CHICORY AND ASPARAGUS SALAD

SERVES I

75 g (3 oz) thin asparagus, trimmed
salt
I small head of chicory, broken into individual
 leaves
25 g (I oz) fresh Parmesan cheese, grated
sprigs fresh thyme, to garnish (optional)
I small brown roll, to serve

1. Cook the asparagus in boiling salted water
for 2–3 minutes, or until just tender.
2. Place the chicory on a flameproof serving
dish. Drain the asparagus and place on top of
the chicory.
3. Sprinkle over the Parmesan cheese. Place the
dish under a medium grill for 2–3 minutes until
the cheese starts to melt. Garnish with fresh
thyme. Serve with a brown roll and Vinaigrette
Dressing.

VINAIGRETTE DRESSING

MAKES 200-250 ml (7-9 fl oz)

175-225 ml (6-8 fl oz) olive oil
3 × 15 ml tbs white wine, red wine or
 herb vinegar
½ × 5 ml tsp caster sugar or honey
2 × 5 ml tsp Dijon mustard
salt and pepper

Whisk together all the ingredients until
combined. Season with salt and pepper.

VARIATIONS

Herb Whisk into the dressing 2 × 15 ml tbs
finely chopped, fresh mixed herbs, such as
parsley, thyme, marjoram, chives, sage.
Mustard and Parsley Stir in 1 × 15 ml tbs

wholegrain mustard and 2 × 15 ml tbs finely
chopped fresh parsley.
Sweet and Spiced Add 1 × 5 ml tsp mango
chutney, 1 × 5 ml tsp mild curry paste and
½ × 5 ml tsp ground turmeric.
Roquefort Place the dressing in a blender or
food processor. Add 25 g (1 oz) Roquefort
cheese and 2 × 15 ml tbs single cream. Blend
until smooth.
Garlic Crush 1–2 garlic cloves into the
dressing.

SUMMER PLATTER

SERVES 4-6

900 g (2 lb) small new potatoes
salt
900 g (2 lb) asparagus, well trimmed
12 large cooked prawns with shells
12 radishes
I packet of bread-sticks
150 ml (5 fl oz) soured cream
I × 15 ml tbs chopped fresh herbs
fresh chives, to garnish
115 g (4 oz) black or red lumpfish caviar

1. Boil the potatoes in salted water until just
tender. Drain well, then leave to cool.
2. Meanwhile, blanch the asparagus in boiling,
salted water until just tender. Drain well and
refresh under cold water.
3. Arrange the potatoes, asparagus, prawns,
radishes and bread-sticks on a large platter.
4. Mix the soured cream with the herbs in a
small bowl. Garnish with chives. Serve the
vegetable platter and soured cream dip
together. Let guests help themselves to the
lumpfish caviar. If time allows, cut the potatoes
in half, spread each half with some soured
cream and top with a little lumpfish caviar.

Warm Salad with Bacon

SERVES 4

½ head of endive, broken into small pieces
I small radicchio lettuce, separated into leaves
25 g (1 oz) lamb's lettuce or roquette
225 g (8 oz) streaky bacon, rind removed and cut
    into 2.5 cm (1 in) strips about 0.6 cm (¼ in) wide
3 × 15 ml tbs walnut oil
I × 15 ml tbs red wine vinegar
½ × 5 ml tsp mild wholegrain mustard
salt and pepper
fried bread croûtons, to garnish

I. Wash and dry all the salad leaves. Divide the endive, radicchio leaves and lamb's lettuce or roquette leaves between four plates.
2. Fry the bacon strips in a small frying pan over moderate heat until the fat runs, then continue frying until the strips are crisp and brown, stirring occasionally.
3. Pour off the excess fat from the frying pan, then add the walnut oil, vinegar, mustard and seasoning to the bacon. Heat gently for 30 seconds, scraping the base of the pan, then spoon the bacon and dressing over the salads. Toss the leaves with the bacon and dressing, garnish with croûtons and serve at once.

Warm Salad with Bacon

Chick-Pea and Artichoke Heart Salad

SERVES 6

4 × 15 ml tbs grapeseed oil
4 × 5 ml tsp red wine vinegar
1 × 5 ml tsp wholegrain mustard
3 × 15 ml tbs chopped fresh parsley
430 g can chick-peas, drained and rinsed
400 g can whole artichoke hearts, drained, halved
    and rinsed
salt and pepper

1. To make the dressing, place the oil, red wine vinegar, wholegrain mustard and chopped parsley in a large bowl and whisk together.
2. Stir in the chick-peas, artichokes and seasoning. Cover with clingfilm and chill until ready to serve. Stir again before serving.

VARIATION Replace the chick-peas with well-drained canned butter beans, broad beans or kidney beans.

Warm Salmon Salad

SERVES 4

75 ml (3 fl oz) oil
2 × 15 ml tbs orange juice
1 × 5 ml tbs clear honey
seeds of 1 green cardamom pod, crushed
finely grated rind of 1 lemon
2 × 5 ml tsp lemon juice
4 salmon steaks, about 150 g (5 oz) each
a mixture of green salad leaves
fresh orange segments (optional)

1. Put 50 ml (2 fl oz) of the oil, the orange juice, honey, cardamom seeds and the lemon rind and juice in a bowl and whisk together.
2. Place the salmon in a non-metallic dish and

pour over the citrus marinade. Cover and marinate in the refrigerator overnight.
3. Drain the salmon, reserving the marinade. Brush the salmon steaks with the remaining oil. Cook under a hot grill for about 8 minutes, turning once, until the flesh flakes easily.
4. Heat reserved marinade in a pan. Toss with the salad leaves.
5. Serve the salmon with the warm salad. Or, break salmon into large chunks, toss into the salad, with the orange segments if using, and serve immediately.

Warm Livers with Bitter Leaves

SERVES 2

25 g (1 oz) butter
225 g (8 oz) chicken livers, well trimmed
25 g (1 oz) onion, skinned and roughly chopped
1 small garlic clove, skinned and crushed
8 × 15 ml tbs red wine
1-2 × 5 ml tsp cider vinegar
1 × 15 ml tbs whole cranberry sauce
salt and pepper
1 small radicchio lettuce, separated into leaves, or
    a mixture of bitter leaves

1. Melt the butter in a large frying pan and cook the whole livers with the onion and garlic over fairly high heat, turning once, until crisp and brown. Remove and keep warm.
2. Pour the wine, 1 × 5 ml tsp of the vinegar and the cranberry sauce into the pan. Boil for 1 minute to reduce. Stir to include the crispy brown bits on the base of the pan.
3. Check seasoning, adding extra vinegar, if needed. The texture should be slightly syrupy.
4. Arrange the leaves on two plates. Top with the livers, pour over the hot dressing and serve.

Warm Salmon Salad

Bean and Tuna Salad

SERVES 3-4

175 g (6 oz) frozen French green beans
115 g (4 oz) onion, skinned and thinly sliced
400 g can flageolet beans or 430 g can chick-peas,
    drained and rinsed
2 × 15 ml tbs olive oil
2 × 5 ml tsp white wine vinegar
salt and pepper
200 g can tuna fish, drained and flaked
chopped fresh parsley (optional)
granary bread, to serve

1. Cook the beans in boiling salted water until just tender. Drain and cool under cold running water. Halve if large.
2. Place the onion in a saucepan of cold water. Bring to the boil, then simmer for 2 minutes. Drain and cool under cold running water.
3. Place the French beans and onion in a bowl with the flageolet beans or chick-peas. Add the oil, vinegar and seasoning.
4. Add the tuna to the bowl. Toss lightly to mix. Sprinkle with fresh chopped parsley. Serve with thick chunks of granary bread.

Garlic Croûton Salad

SERVES 1

25 g (1 oz) French bread, cut into thin slices
1 garlic clove, skinned and halved
40 g (1½ oz) garlic and herb soft cheese
mixture of salad leaves
salt and pepper

1. Toast the bread slices on both sides.
2. Rub one side of each slice with the cut garlic, then spread the soft cheese on this side. Grill gently until the cheese browns slightly.
3. Arrange the salad leaves on a plate and place the croûtons on top. Season and serve at once.

Peasant Salad

SERVES 8

675 g (1½ lb) potatoes, scrubbed
salt
450 g (1 lb) asparagus (or 1 large bundle),
    trimmed
3 eggs, hard-boiled
1 avocado
2 small red onions, skinned, halved and thinly
    sliced
1 red pepper, seeded and chopped
1 yellow pepper, seeded and chopped
chopped fresh parsley
2 courgettes, trimmed and very thinly sliced
50 g (2 oz) green or black olives
3 × 15 ml tbs capers
3 × 15 ml tbs mayonnaise
1 quantity Mustard and Parsley Dressing
    (see page 18)

1. Cook the potatoes in boiling salted water for about 15 minutes or until tender.
2. Steam the asparagus (see Cook's Tip).
3. Drain the potatoes. Leave to cool slightly, then peel off the skins, if preferred. Cut the potatoes into large chunks. Cut off the asparagus tips and reserve. Chop the stems into 2.5 cm (1 in) pieces. Shell the eggs and cut into wedges. Peel and stone the avocado, and cut the flesh into chunks.
4. Mix all the ingredients together in a serving bowl. Whisk the mayonnaise into the dressing and pour over the salad. Toss together and serve immediately.

COOK'S TIP The best way to steam asparagus is to stand it, tied in a bundle, tips upwards, in about 5 cm (2 in) of simmering salted water in a pan. Cover the tips with a tent of foil and cook for 5-8 minutes.

Smoky Bean Salad

SERVES 6

450 g (1 lb) smoked haddock fillet, skinned
a little milk and water
430 g can borlotti beans, drained and
   rinsed
150 ml (5 fl oz) soured cream
1-2 × 5 ml tsp curry paste
3-4 × 15 ml tbs lemon juice
3 × 15 ml tbs chopped fresh parsley
black pepper
mixture of salad leaves
3 eggs, hard-boiled and quartered
fresh herbs, to garnish

1. Put the fish in a large frying pan and cover
with milk and water. Bring to the boil, then
simmer, covered, for about 5 minutes, or until
tender. Drain, discarding any small bones, and
break the fish into large flakes. Add the beans
to the fish.
2. To make a dressing, combine the soured
cream, curry paste, lemon juice and parsley in a
bowl. Season with pepper. Lightly fold the
dressing into the haddock mixture.
3. Serve on a bed of salad leaves, garnished
with hard-boiled egg quarters, freshly ground
pepper and herbs.

VARIATION Try canned butter or cannellini
beans instead of borlotti beans.

Peasant Salad

Mediterranean Salad

SERVES 8

4 × 15 ml tbs olive oil
2 × 15 ml tbs lemon juice or white wine vinegar
1 × 15 ml tbs wholegrain mustard
salt and pepper
1 mild onion, skinned and finely sliced
2 × 430 g cans butter beans, drained and rinsed
1 salad onion, finely sliced
½ red pepper, seeded and very finely diced
200 g can tuna fish in brine, drained and roughly
  flaked
115 g (4 oz) stuffed green olives, sliced
3 × 15 ml tbs chopped fresh coriander or parsley
  (optional)

1. To make the dressing, whisk together the oil, lemon juice or vinegar, wholegrain mustard and seasoning in a large bowl.
2. Stir in the onion, butter beans, salad onion and red pepper. Stir these around in the dressing, then spoon on to a serving platter.
3. Scatter the tuna fish over the beans. Finish with the olives and the coriander. Cover and refrigerate until required.

COOK'S TIP For an authentic Mediterranean flavour, serve this salad with well-drained anchovy fillets arranged over the top in a lattice pattern. Quartered hard-boiled eggs also go well with this salad.

'Hot' Red Salad with Garlic Prawns

SERVES 6

DRESSING:
50 ml (2 fl oz) balsamic vinegar
150 ml (5 fl oz) olive oil
½ × 5 ml tsp caster sugar
2 garlic cloves, skinned and crushed
salt and pepper
2 small red chillies, finely chopped
SALAD:
115 g (4 oz) cooked peeled prawns
juice of 1 orange
2 oranges, peeled and thinly sliced
150 g (5 oz) small cooked beetroot
  (see Cook's Tip), thinly sliced
1 head of radicchio lettuce, separated into
  individual leaves
1 head of chicory, preferably red, separated into
  individual leaves
chopped fresh dill, to garnish

1. To make the dressing, whisk together all the dressing ingredients. Stir in the prawns.
2. Toss together the orange juice, orange slices and beetroot slices. You will find the orange takes on the ruby red colour of the beetroot.
3. Arrange the radicchio and chicory leaves in a shallow salad bowl. Using a slotted spoon, drain the orange slices and beetroot from the juice and scatter over the leaves. Drain the prawns and scatter over the top.
4. Mix together the beetroot juices and dressing and spoon a little over the salad. Serve the remainder separately. Garnish salad with dill.

COOK'S TIP Look for vacuum packs of cooked beetroot in their own juices, which are excellent.

'Hot' Red Salad with Garlic Prawns

QUICK MUFFIN PIZZAS

SERVES 4

4 plain muffins, split
butter or margarine
3 × 15 ml tbs tomato ketchup
200 g can tuna fish, drained and flaked
salt and pepper
115 g (4 oz) Mozzarella cheese, thinly sliced
8 black olives, stoned

1. Lightly toast the muffins on both sides.
Spread the insides with butter and ketchup.
2. Place the tuna on top and season.
3. Place the Mozzarella on top of the tuna to
cover. Top with the olives. Grill until the
cheese melts and is bubbly. Serve immediately.

SALAMI AND CHEESE PIZZA

SERVES 4

2 × 175 g (6 oz) packet deep pan pizza mix
1 × 5 ml tsp dried mixed herbs
salt and pepper
25 g (1 oz) Cheddar cheese, grated
3 × 15 ml tbs pesto sauce
3 × 15 ml tbs tomato ketchup
115 g (4 oz) salami, roughly chopped
2 medium tomatoes, sliced
115 g (4 oz) Mozzarella cheese, sliced

1. Make the pizza dough according to packet
instructions, adding the herbs, a pinch of salt
and the Cheddar cheese. Knead, then press into
a 26 × 16.5 cm (10 ¼ × 6 ½ in) shallow tin.
2. Spread the pesto then tomato ketchup over
the base, then add the salami and tomatoes.
Arrange Mozzarella on top and season.
3. Bake at 220°C/425°F/Gas Mark 7 for 12-15
minutes. Allow to cool, then cut into fingers.

Quick Muffin Pizzas

ROASTED PEPPER AND SWEET ONION PIZZA

SERVES 6

4 large yellow or red peppers
olive oil
4 large white or red onions, skinned and sliced
3 long-life pizza bases, about 23 cm (9 in) in
   diameter
2 × 200 g (7 oz) Mozzarella cheeses, sliced
2 × 400 g cans chopped tomatoes, well drained
6 garlic cloves, skinned and thinly sliced
salt and freshly ground pepper
4 × 15 ml tbs chopped fresh oregano or basil
   leaves

1. Grill the peppers until blackened. Cover
with a damp cloth and leave until cool enough
to handle. Carefully peel off the skins. Remove
and discard the stalks and seeds. Cut the flesh
into thick strips.
2. Heat 4 × 15 ml tbs olive oil in a frying pan,
and fry the onions gently for 5 minutes until
softened but not coloured.
3. Place the pizza bases on baking sheets and
lightly brush with olive oil.
4. Cover the pizza bases with the Mozzarella
cheese. Scatter over the tomatoes, onions and
peppers, then the slivers of garlic. Season with
salt and pepper, drizzle with olive oil and brush
the edges of the pizza with oil. Bake in the
oven at 220°C/425°F Gas Mark 7 for 15–20
minutes, scattering the herbs over the top 5
minutes before the pizzas are cooked. Serve
immediately.

CHORIZO, FETA AND AUBERGINE PIZZA

SERVES 2

2 long-life pizza bases, about 23 cm (9 in)
   in diameter
50 ml (2 fl oz) olive oil
450 g (1 lb) tomatoes, sliced
1 small aubergine, about 175 g (6 oz), thinly sliced
150 g (5 oz) chorizo or other spicy sausage, cut
   into chunks
115 g (4 oz) feta cheese
1 × 15 ml tbs roughly chopped fresh oregano or
   parsley
pepper
oregano leaves, to garnish (optional)

1. Place the pizza bases on baking sheets and
lightly brush with olive oil. Scatter the
tomatoes over the bases up to the edges. Tuck
the aubergine slices between the tomatoes.
2. Scatter the chorizo over the pizzas. Top
with crumbled feta and sprinkle over the
oregano. Season with pepper only as feta is
salty. Drizzle with the remaining olive oil.
3. Bake in the oven at 220°C/425°F/Gas
Mark 7 for 15-20 minutes. Serve immediately,
garnished with fresh oregano leaves or parsley
sprigs if you like.

COOK'S TIP Vacuum-packed pizza bases
from the supermarket make this a really speedy
recipe.

Chorizo, Feta and Aubergine Pizza

CREAMY VEGETABLE PASTA

SERVES 2-3

25 g (1 oz) walnut pieces
175 g (6 oz) tagliatelle or spaghetti
salt and pepper
175 g (6 oz) courgettes, thinly sliced
175 g (6 oz) frozen broad beans
150 g (5 oz) full-fat soft cheese with garlic and
  herbs
about 4 × 15 ml tbs milk or single cream

1. Toast the walnut pieces in a dry frying pan over medium heat, stirring.
2. Place the pasta in a large saucepan of boiling salted water and return to the boil. After about 3 minutes, add the courgettes and beans. After 7 more minutes, when the pasta is tender and the beans cooked, drain well.
3. Return the pasta and vegetables to the saucepan and heat gently. Stir in the cheese and milk, adding more milk if necessary to make a smooth sauce. Season. Serve straightaway with walnut pieces sprinkled over the top for garnish.

PASTA WITH PEPERAMI

SERVES 2

225 g (8 oz) dried tagliatelle or fettucine
salt and pepper
50 g (2 oz) red pepper, seeded and very thinly
  sliced
115 g (4 oz) cucumber, halved, seeded and sliced
2 × 15 ml tbs chopped fresh parsley
1 × 15 ml tbs French dressing
50 g (2 oz) peperami (salami stick), sliced
grated Parmesan or Cheddar cheese, to serve

1. Place the pasta in a large saucepan of boiling salted water and cook until just tender, adding the pepper and cucumber for the last minute.

2. Drain the pasta and put in a large serving bowl. Stir in the parsley, then fold in the dressing with the peperami. Season to taste. Serve at once sprinkled with the cheese.

PASTA WITH SAUTÉED MUSHROOMS

SERVES 2-3

335 g (12 oz) dried pasta
salt and pepper
4 × 15 ml tbs olive oil
335 g (12 oz) open-cup or oyster mushrooms,
  wiped and thickly sliced
1 garlic clove, skinned and crushed
large knob of butter
2 × 15 ml tbs chopped fresh herbs
4 × 15 ml tbs double cream (optional)
freshly grated Parmesan cheese, to serve
sprigs of fresh herbs, to garnish

1. Place the pasta in a large saucepan of boiling salted water and cook until just tender.
2. Meanwhile, heat the oil in a frying pan and fry the mushrooms for 3-4 minutes until slightly browned. Lower the heat, add the garlic and continue cooking the mushrooms until the pasta is cooked.
3. Drain the pasta and return to the saucepan with the butter and plenty of black pepper.
4. Season the mushrooms and add the herbs and cream, if using. Tip the pasta on to serving plates, top with the mushrooms and serve with Parmesan cheese and herb sprigs to garnish.

VARIATION Core, seed and very thinly slice 1 red, green or yellow pepper. Heat 4 × 15 tbs olive oil and fry the pepper strips over high heat until softened. Stir in herbs to taste and proceed with the recipe above.

Pasta with Sautéed Mushrooms

PASTA WITH BACON SAUCE

SERVES 4

335 g (12 oz) dried pasta, such as vermicelli,
    spaghetti or quills
salt and pepper
4 × 15 ml tbs olive oil
2 garlic cloves, skinned and crushed
225 g (8 oz) smoked streaky bacon,
    rind removed and chopped
2 × 400 g cans chopped tomatoes
115 g (4 oz) black olives, stoned
4 × 15 ml tbs chopped fresh herbs, such as basil,
    marjoram or parsley
fresh chopped herbs, to garnish

1. Place the pasta in a large saucepan of boiling
salted water and cook until just tender.
2. Drain the pasta well and toss with 2 × 15
ml tbs of the olive oil. Cover and keep warm.
3. Meanwhile, heat the remaining oil in a
frying pan and fry the garlic and bacon until
golden. Stir in the tomatoes, olives and herbs
and cook for 2-3 minutes. Adjust seasoning.
4. Toss the bacon sauce with the hot pasta and
leave, covered, for 1 minute. Toss pasta again
and serve garnished with extra herbs.

EGG AND BACON PILAFF

SERVES 4

2 × 15 ml tbs oil
115 g (4 oz) streaky bacon, rinded and
    cut into bite-sized pieces
115 g (4 oz) onion, skinned and thinly sliced
175 g (6 oz) long-grain white rice
½ × 5 ml tsp ground turmeric
300 ml (10 fl oz) vegetable or chicken stock
salt and pepper
150 ml (5 fl oz) dry cider
4 eggs
chopped fresh parsley, to garnish

1. Heat the oil in a shallow, flameproof
casserole or deep frying pan and fry the bacon
and onion until golden brown. Stir in rice and
turmeric and cook for about 1 minute.
2. Add the stock and seasoning and bring to the
boil, stirring. Cover and simmer gently for
about 10 minutes.
3. Pour the cider into the casserole and adjust
seasoning to taste. Make small hollows in the
rice. Break each egg into a cup, then tip
carefully into the hollows.
4. Cover the casserole or pan and continue to
simmer for a further 7-8 minutes, or until the
eggs are just set, adding a little more stock if
necessary. Serve garnished with parsley.

LEEK AND LENTIL PILAFF

SERVES 4

1–2 × 15 ml tbs oil
450 g (1 lb) leeks, split, thickly sliced
    rinsed and drained
115 g (4 oz) blanched almonds, split
2 × 5 ml tsp ground coriander
175 g (6 oz) long-grain white rice
115 g (4 oz) split red lentils, boiled rapidly for
    10 minutes then drained
750-900 ml (25-30 fl oz) vegetable stock
1 garlic clove, skinned and crushed
salt and pepper

1. Heat the oil in a medium saucepan and fry
the leeks and almonds for 3-5 minutes until
starting to brown, stirring.
2. Stir in the ground coriander and cook for 1
minute, stirring occasionally.
3. Stir in the rice, lentils, stock, garlic and
seasoning. Bring to the boil, then cover and
simmer for 15-20 minutes or until the rice is
tender and most of the stock is absorbed. Serve
at once.

Pasta with Bacon Sauce

PAELLA WITH PEPPERS

SERVES 6

1–2 × 15 ml tbs oil
175 g (6 oz) onion, skinned and thinly sliced
1 small red pepper, seeded and chopped
1 small green pepper, seeded and chopped
1 small yellow pepper, seeded and chopped
225 g (8 oz) chicken breast fillet, chopped
275 g (10 oz) long-grain white rice
600 ml (20 fl oz) chicken stock
225 g (8 oz) ripe tomatoes, skinned, seeded and
  chopped
finely grated rind and juice of 1 lemon
pinch of saffron threads
335 g (12 oz) fish fillet, skinned and chopped
225 g (8 oz) ready-to-eat seafood cocktail
115 g (4 oz) frozen peas
salt and pepper
lemon wedges and fresh parsley, to garnish

1. Heat oil in a large sauté pan or flameproof casserole and fry the onion and peppers for 3-4 minutes until softened.
2. Using a slotted spoon, remove the vegetables, then add the chicken and the rice, with a little more oil if necessary. Cook, stirring, for 1-2 minutes.
3. Return the vegetables to the pan with the stock, tomatoes, lemon rind and juice and a pinch of saffron. Bring to the boil and boil for 1 minute, then reduce the heat and add the fish. Season to taste.
4. Cover and simmer for about 15 minutes, or until the rice is almost tender, adding more stock if necessary (there should be little free liquid).
5. Stir seafood cocktail and peas into the rice. Cover the pan tightly and cook for a further 2-3 minutes or until all the fish is heated through. Adjust the seasoning, garnish and serve immediately.

Paella with Peppers

MUSHROOM AND PARMESAN RISOTTO

SERVES 4

225 g (8 oz) broccoli florets
175 g (6 oz) French beans topped and tailed and
  halved lengthways
salt and pepper
2 × 15 ml tbs olive oil
115 g (4 oz) onion, skinned and finely chopped
335 g (12 oz) arborio rice
pinch of saffron threads (optional)
4 × 15 ml tbs dry white wine
pared rind of 1 lemon
2 × 15 ml tbs lemon juice
750 ml (25 fl oz) vegetable stock
175 g (6 oz) flat mushrooms, wiped and sliced
freshly grated Parmesan cheese, to serve

1. Blanch the broccoli florets and French beans in a large saucepan of boiling salted water for about 4 minutes. Drain and refresh under cold running water. Set aside.
2. Heat the oil in a flameproof casserole and fry the onion for about 2-3 minutes until starting to soften. Stir in the rice and saffron, if using, and season well. Pour in the wine, lemon rind, juice and stock.
3. Bring to the boil, stirring, then cover and simmer for 5 minutes. Stir in the mushrooms, broccoli and French beans.
4. Re-cover and simmer for a further 5 minutes, or until the rice is almost tender and most of the liquid absorbed. Remove the lemon rind and serve immediately with grated Parmesan cheese.

COOK'S TIP This is a wonderfully warming meal for a cold night. Look out for Italian risotto rice (arborio) in the supermarket. You can also stir in some cooked prawns or mussels. Make sure you pare the lemon rind in one large piece, so it's easy to remove.

Glazed Chicken Rice Casserole

SERVES 4

finely grated rind of I orange
finely grated rind of I lemon
2 × 15 ml tbs orange juice
I × 15 ml tbs lemon juice
2 × 15 ml tbs clear honey
¼ × 5 ml tsp turmeric
12 boned and skinned chicken thighs, about 450 g
(I lb) total weight
2 × 15 ml tbs oil
50 g (2 oz) salad onions, thinly sliced with a few
green tops reserved for garnish
115 g (4 oz) long-grain white rice, preferably
basmati
300 ml (10 fl oz) chicken stock
salt and pepper

1. Mix together the orange and lemon rinds
and juices, the honey and turmeric. Add the
chicken and stir to coat completely.
2. Heat the oil in a medium sauté pan and
brown the chicken pieces, a few at a time,
reserving the leftover honey mixture. Take
care as the chicken splutters while it is
browning.
3. Return all the chicken to the pan. Add the
remaining ingredients and any excess glaze.
Bring to the boil, then cover and simmer for
about 15 minutes or until the rice and chicken
are tender and most of the excess liquid
absorbed.
4. Adjust seasoning and serve immediately,
garnished with salad onion tops.

Chinese Rice Pot

SERVES 4

225 g (8 oz) mixed wild and long-grain rice
3 × 15 ml tbs olive oil
I cm (½ in) piece fresh root ginger, peeled
and finely chopped
2 garlic cloves, skinned and finely chopped
450 g (I lb) skinless chicken breast fillets
salt and pepper
about 600 ml (20 fl oz) chicken or vegetable stock
335 g (12 oz) broccoli, cut into small florets
225 g (8 oz) fresh asparagus or young leeks,
trimmed, cut into 2.5 cm (I in) pieces,
rinsed and drained
2 × 5 ml tsp sesame oil
fresh herbs and grated lemon rind, to garnish

1. Place the rice in a sieve and rinse under cold
running water until the water runs clear.
2. Heat the olive oil in a large heavy saucepan
preferably non-stick, and stir-fry the ginger,
garlic and chicken for 2-3 minutes until
beginning to brown.
3. Add the rice, salt and pepper to taste and stir
well. Pour in enough stock to cover
completely and bring quickly to the boil. Place
the broccoli and asparagus or leeks on top of
the rice. Cover tightly and leave to simmer
gently for 10 minutes.
4. Stir quickly to mix the vegetables through
the rice. Cover tightly again and leave to cook
for a further 10 minutes.
5. Fluff up the rice, sprinkle with sesame oil
and garnish with herbs and lemon rind.

COOK'S TIP'S It's important to rinse the rice
to help remove the starch.
You can substitute any fresh vegetables for
the broccoli and asparagus – try French beans,
carrots or peas. If you like crisp vegetables,
don't stir them through the rice (step 4); leave
them to steam over it for the 20 minutes
cooking time.

Aubergine Risotto

SERVES 2

335 g (12 oz) aubergine, halved
3 × 15 ml tbs olive oil
2 garlic cloves, skinned and crushed
115 g (4 oz) onion, skinned and chopped
175 g (6 oz) mixed wild and long-grain rice
1 × 5 ml tsp tomato purée
600 ml (20 fl oz) vegetable stock
50 g (2 oz) salted peanuts, chopped
1 × 15 ml tbs chopped fresh basil
salt and pepper

1. Grill the aubergine, skin side uppermost, for 7-10 minutes, or until the skin wrinkles. Peel and chop the flesh into 2 cm (¾ in) cubes.
2. Heat the oil in a large sauté pan and fry the

Chinese Rice Pot

garlic, onion and aubergines. Cook, stirring, for 2 minutes, then mix in the rice, tomato purée and stock.
3. Bring to the boil, then cover and simmer for 20 minutes or until the rice is tender. Stir in the peanuts, basil and seasoning and serve immediately.

COOK'S TIP Look for packets of mixed wild and long-grain. Wild rice, in fact, is aquatic grass, not a rice at all. Traditionally, it is harvested by hand in North America. It adds extra texture and a slight nutty flavour to this dish. You can use all long-grain rice instead, if preferred.

AUBERGINE AND BEAN GRATIN

SERVES 4

2 medium aubergines, ends cut off
15 g (½ oz) butter or margarine
I onion, skinned and chopped
I garlic clove, skinned and crushed
115 g (4 oz) button mushrooms, wiped
   and trimmed
½ × 430 g can cannellini beans, drained
   and rinsed
2 tomatoes, chopped
pepper
2 × 15 ml tbs freshly grated **Parmesan cheese**
fresh parsley sprigs, to garnish

1. Place the aubergines in a saucepan of boiling water and cook for about 10 minutes, or until tender. Drain well.
2. Cut the aubergines in half lengthways and scoop out the flesh, leaving 0.6 cm (¼ in) shells. Finely chop the flesh and reserve the shells.
3. Melt the butter or margarine in a saucepan and gently cook the onion, garlic and chopped aubergine flesh for 5 minutes, stirring. Add the mushrooms, beans, tomatoes and pepper to taste.
4. Stuff the aubergine shells with the bean mixture and sprinkle with Parmesan cheese. Place under a hot grill for 4–5 minutes, or until heated through. Serve hot, garnished with fresh parsley.

Aubergine and Bean Gratin

CAULIFLOWER GRATIN WITH PARSLEY SAUCE

SERVES 3-4

450 g (I lb) cauliflower, cut into florets, or
 frozen cauliflower florets
salt and pepper
21 g packet parsley sauce mix
600 ml (20 fl oz) milk
75 g (3 oz) butter or margarine, diced
115 g (4 oz) plain wholemeal flour
50 g (2 oz) porridge oats
75 g (3 oz) Cheddar cheese, grated

1. Place the cauliflower florets in a saucepan of
boiling salted water and cook until just tender.
Drain well and place in a shallow ovenproof
serving dish.
2. Make up the parsley sauce according to
packet instructions. Pour over the cauliflower.
3. Rub or fork the fat into the flour until
evenly blended. Stir in the oats and cheese and
spoon over the dish.
4. Bake in the oven at 200°C/400°F/Gas
Mark 6 for about 20 minutes, or until golden
brown and bubbling. Serve immediately.

COOK'S TIP If the packet sauce mix seems a
little thick, stir in extra milk to thin it down.

COD AND CRAB GRATIN

SERVES 4

about 675 g (1½ lb) medium-sized new potatoes,
 well scrubbed
450 g (I lb) cod fillet, skinned and cut into
 2.5 cm (I in) cubes
300 ml (10 fl oz) milk
salt and pepper
225 g (8 oz) small button mushrooms, wiped
 and trimmed
40 g (1½ oz) butter
40 g (1½ oz) plain flour
115 g (4 oz) each white and dark crab meat
2 × 5 ml tsp Dijon mustard
75 g (3 oz) Cheddar cheese, grated

1. Boil the potatoes in their skins until tender.
Drain, then slice thickly.
2. Meanwhile, place the cod in a saucepan with
the milk and seasoning. Bring to the boil, then
cover and simmer for 5 minutes.
3. Add the mushrooms, re-cover and simmer
for a further 5 minutes or until the fish is
tender and the flesh flakes easily when tested
with the tip of a knife. Strain off and reserve
the milk.
4. Place the fish and mushrooms in a shallow
flameproof serving dish, cover and keep warm.
5. Put the butter, flour and reserved milk in a
saucepan. Heat, whisking continuously, until
sauce thickens, boils and is smooth. Simmer for
2-3 minutes.
6. Stir in the crab meat, mustard and seasoning
and heat gently until thoroughly hot. Pour
over the cod and mushrooms, stirring gently to
mix. Level the surface with a knife.
7. Top with thick potato slices and scatter over
the Cheddar cheese. Grill until golden and
bubbling. Serve immediately.

VARIATION If you wish you can top the dish
with crisps in place of the new potatoes for a
crunchier topping.

Chicory and Carrot Gratin

SERVES 4

175 g (6 oz) carrots, peeled and thickly sliced
salt and pepper
4 heads chicory, cored and thickly sliced
150 ml (5 fl oz) soured cream
½ garlic clove, skinned and crushed

1. Place the carrots in a large saucepan of boiling salted water and cook for about 6 minutes, or until just tender. Drain well.

2. Mix together all the ingredients and place in a flameproof serving dish. Season well with salt and plenty of black pepper.

3. Place under a moderate grill for 10 minutes, then turn the heat to high for a further 2 minutes to brown. Serve immediately on its own or with warm bread.

COOK'S TIP This is good with grilled meat, fish or on its own with warm bread, such as garlic focaccia from the delicatessen counter. Alternatively, split open a French stick, drizzle with olive oil and garlic. Toast and serve warm.

Chicory and Carrot Gratin

Vegetable and Cheese Croûtes

SERVES 4

2 garlic cloves, skinned and crushed
150 ml (5 fl oz) olive oil
1 × 5 ml tsp chopped fresh thyme, or
  ½ × 5 ml tsp dried
salt and pepper
1 small aubergine, thinly sliced
1 medium courgette, cut into 1 cm (½ in) slices
1 small bulb fennel, trimmed and chopped
1 small red pepper, seeded and cut into 8 pieces
1 small yellow pepper, seeded and cut into
  8 pieces
4 large thick slices white crusty bread
115 g (4 oz) halloumi, feta or another mild
  crumbly goat's cheese
chopped fresh herbs, to garnish

1. Mix the garlic with the oil and herbs and season well. Stir in the vegetables, cover and leave to marinate for at least 10 minutes, preferably longer.
2. Spread the vegetables over a foil-lined grill pan. Grill for 15 minutes, turning at least 3 times and basting with the oil. Cover and keep warm.
3. Brush the bread on both sides with olive oil from the bottom of the grill pan and toast lightly.
4. Place a layer of sliced halloumi over one side of the toasted bread, pile the vegetables on top and finish with the remaining cheese. Place under the grill for 2-3 minutes until bubbling. Serve immediately, garnished with herbs.

COOK'S TIP Halloumi is a hard, salty Cypriot ewe's-milk cheese. It can also be made from cow's milk, which gives a slightly softer cheese. Sold in vacuum packs bathed in a little water and mint, it doesn't lose its shape when cooked and can be grilled or fried in slices.

Cheese and Chive Mushrooms

SERVES 2-3

1 × 15 ml tbs oil
115 g (4 oz) onion, skinned and roughly chopped
225 g (8 oz) minced pork
295 g can condensed cream of mushroom soup
3 × 15 ml tbs chopped fresh chives
pepper
4 large flat mushrooms, about 335 g (12 oz) total
  weight, wiped
150 ml (5 fl oz) milk
75 g (3 oz) Cheddar cheese, grated

1. Heat the oil in a medium saucepan and fry the onion until golden, stirring occasionally. Add the pork and continue to cook over a high heat for 3-4 minutes, stirring all the time. Pour off any excess fat.
2. Add half the soup and the chives. Stir over a gentle heat for 1-2 minutes. Season to taste.
3. Place the mushrooms in a single layer in a shallow ovenproof dish. Divide the pork mixture among the mushrooms.
4. Whisk together the milk and remaining soup and pour over the mushrooms. Sprinkle the Cheddar cheese on top.
5. Bake in the oven at 200°C/400°F/Gas Mark 6 for 25-30 minutes. Serve immediately.

Vegetable and Cheese Croûtes

Chick-Pea and Mushroom Bake

SERVES 3-4

430 g can chick-peas, drained and rinsed
½ × 295 g can condensed cream of mushroom
    soup
salt and pepper
3 eggs, separated
butter or margarine for greasing dish
200 g can artichoke hearts, drained and quartered
coarse oatmeal for sprinkling over top

1. Purée the chick-peas with the soup and
plenty of seasoning in a blender or food
processor. When almost smooth, add the egg
yolks and blend for a few seconds only.
2. Lightly grease a shallow ovenproof serving
dish. Scatter the artichokes in the dish.
3. Whisk the egg whites until stiff but not dry.
Fold in the chick-pea mixture. Turn into the
dish and sprinkle with a little oatmeal.
4. Bake in the oven at 200°C/400°F/Gas
Mark 6 for 20-30 minutes, or until golden.
Serve immediately.

VARIATION This easy supper dish can be
made with a variety of other canned pulses,
such as butter beans, haricot beans, kidney
beans or borlotti beans and other canned
condensed soup such as cream of tomato of
cream of asparagus.

30-Minute Chicken and Artichoke Bake

SERVES 4

50 g (2 oz) butter, plus extra for brushing filo
    pastry
4 x 15 ml tbs plain flour
450 ml (16 fl oz) milk
75 g (3 oz) Cheddar cheese, grated
675 g (1½ lb) cooked boneless chicken, skinned
    and cut into bite-sized pieces
400 g can artichoke hearts, drained and halved
finely grated rind of 1 lemon
1-2 × 15 ml tbs lemon juice
2 × 15 ml tbs chopped fresh herbs, such as parsley
    or chives
salt and pepper
4 sheets filo pastry, thawed if frozen
25 g (1 oz) sesame seeds

1. Melt 50 g (2 oz) butter, add the flour and
cook, stirring, for 1-2 minutes. Stir in the milk
and simmer for 5 minutes.
2. Add the cheese, chicken, artichoke hearts,
lemon rind and juice to taste, and herbs. Adjust
the seasoning.
3. Spoon the chicken mixture into a 1.5 lt
(2 ½ pt) ovenproof serving dish. Brush the
sheets of filo pastry with a little melted butter
and arrange on top of the chicken.
Alternatively, cut the pastry into thin strips and
scatter roughly over the surface of the chicken.
Scatter over the sesame seeds.
4. Bake in the oven at 220°C/425°F/Gas
Mark 7 for 25 minutes, or until golden brown
and cooked through. Serve immediately.

Cashew-Stuffed Mushrooms

SERVES 4

8 medium flat mushrooms
salt
1 x 15 ml tbs olive oil
2 small onions, skinned and finely chopped
2 garlic cloves, skinned and crushed
50 g (2 oz) unsalted cashew nuts, chopped
1 x 15 ml tbs chopped fresh oregano
2 x 5 ml tsp tomato purée
2-3 x 15 ml tbs grated Parmesan cheese

1. Remove and chop the mushroom stalks. Bring a large pan of salted water to the boil and cook the mushroom caps for 30-60 seconds. Drain and keep warm.

2. Heat the oil in a saucepan and gently fry the onion and garlic for 3-5 minutes or until the onion has softened. Stir in the mushroom stalks, cashew nuts and oregano. Cook for 3-5 minutes until nuts begin to brown. Stir in the tomato purée.

3. Arrange the mushroom caps on an oiled baking tray. Divide the topping between them and sprinkle over the cheese. Bake in the oven at 190°C/375°F/Gas Mark 5 for 10-15 minutes until golden.

30-Minute Chicken and Artichoke Bake

LAMB CHOPS WITH ROSEMARY

SERVES 4

12 large garlic cloves
450 g (1 lb) courgettes, sliced
olive oil for brushing
salt and pepper
4 lamb loin chops, about 175 g (6 oz) each,
    trimmed of fat
long sprigs fresh rosemary

1. Preheat the grill. Boil the unskinned garlic cloves for 5 minutes, drain and arrange in the base of a grill pan with the courgettes. Brush with oil and season.
2. Bend the tail of each chop around the eye of the meat. Using a skewer, make holes through each chop and thread with rosemary sprigs to secure. Brush with oil.
3. Grill garlic and courgettes for 5 minutes, stirring after 2 minutes. Add the lamb and grill for 8 minutes on each side until cooked through but still pink in the centre. The garlic skin will blacken but the flesh will be soft and smoky tasting. Serve immediately.

COOK'S TIP This is the perfect recipe for cooking on the barbecue in the garden on a sunny summer's day. Serve with fresh crusty bread and a green or mixed salad.

Lamb Chops with Rosemary

LAMB NOISETTES WITH MINTED ORANGE SAUCE

SERVES 6

juice of 2 oranges
juice of ½ lemon
1 shallot, skinned and finely chopped
1 bay leaf
2-3 fresh mint sprigs
300 ml (10 fl oz) light meat or vegetable stock
25 g (1 oz) unsalted butter, diced
salt and pepper
1 × 15 ml tbs cornflour
6 large or 12 small lamb noisettes
oil for brushing
pared orange segments and fresh mint sprigs,
    to garnish

1. Place the orange and lemon juices and shallot in a saucepan with the bay leaf, mint sprigs and the stock. Bring to the boil, then partially cover and simmer for 10-15 minutes.
2. Strain the sauce and return to the rinsed-out pan. Whisk the butter into the sauce. Season to taste with salt and pepper.
3. Mix the cornflour with a little cold water to form a smooth paste. Stir into the sauce. Bring to the boil, stirring, and boil for 1-2 minutes, until thickened and smooth. Season.
4. Grill the noisettes for 7-8 minutes on each side, brushing occasionally with a little oil, until cooked through but still pink in the centre.
5. Serve the noisettes in a pool of the orange sauce. Garnish with orange segments and sprigs of fresh mint. Serve immediately.

VARIATION This fresh-tasting, easy-to-make orange sauce is also delicious served with tender chump chops. Grill 6 chops on both sides until the juices run clear when pierced with the tip of a knife.

GOLDEN GRILLED PORK STEAKS

SERVES 4

8 pork loin steaks, about 75 g (3 oz) each
finely grated rind and juice of 1 large orange
3 × 15 ml tbs dry sherry
2 bay leaves
salt and pepper
1 bunch of salad onions, cut into 1 cm (½ in)
    lengths
4 no-soak dried apricots, thinly sliced
2 garlic cloves, skinned and sliced
oil for brushing
300 ml (10 fl oz) chicken stock
1 × 5 ml tsp cornflour
dash of soy sauce
orange slices and fresh herbs, to garnish

1. Trim the loin steaks and curl up into rough rounds, securing each with a cocktail stick. Place in a non-metallic dish.
2. Strain in the orange juice, then add the rind, sherry, bay leaves and seasoning to taste.
3. Scatter the salad onions, apricots and garlic over the pork steaks and stir well to mix. Cover and refrigerate until ready to cook.
4. Lift the pork steaks on to a grill rack. Brush lightly with oil and grill for about 7 minutes each side, or until steaks are tender and well browned. Remove the cocktail sticks.
5. Meanwhile, simmer the marinade ingredients with the stock for 10 minutes. Mix the cornflour with a little water to form a smooth paste. Stir into the pan and boil for 1-2 minutes, stirring all the time. Adjust seasoning and add a dash of soy sauce.
6. To serve, spoon the sauce over the pork steaks; garnish with orange slices and herbs.

COOK'S TIP If steaks are not available, use four 225 g (8 oz) loin chops. Remove the bone, cut in half and continue with step 1.

SIRLOIN STEAKS WITH MUSTARD

SERVES 4

50 g (2 oz) wholegrain mustard
15 g (½ oz) plain flour
4 sirloin steaks, each weighing about 175 g (6 oz)
2 × 15 ml tbs chopped fresh parsley
2 × 15 ml tbs chopped fresh thyme

1. Mix together the mustard and flour, then spread on top of each steak.
2. Line a grill pan with foil, sprinkle with herbs and put the steaks on top. Grill for 5–15 minutes, turning them frequently, until the steaks are cooked to taste. Serve at once.

COOK'S TIP Beef and mustard are a traditional pair. Choose a well-flavoured mustard for this dish, such as Dijon, Meaux or Bordeaux mustard.

Sirloin Steaks with Mustard

SPICED MEATBALLS

MAKES 30

1 large onion, skinned and grated
2 garlic cloves, skinned and crushed
1 green chilli, seeded and chopped
1½ × 5 ml tsp ground cumin
½ × 5 ml tsp mild chilli seasoning
450 g (1 lb) minced lamb
½ × 5 ml tsp salt
½ × 5 ml tsp pepper
grated rind and juice of 1 lemon
olive oil for brushing
fresh thyme sprigs, to garnish

1. Mix together all the ingredients, except the olive oil and thyme.
2. Shape the mixture into 30 small balls, discarding any excess liquid. Brush the grill rack and meatballs lightly with oil.
3. Grill the meatballs for 10–15 minutes under a high heat, turning frequently. Drizzle over a little warm olive oil with thyme and serve.

COOK'S TIP Serve in crusty bread with a cucumber and feta cheese salad.

ITALIAN-STYLE KEBABS

SERVES 4

4 veal escalopes, about 335 g (12 oz) total weight
4 slices smoked ham, each slice cut into 4 strips
4 × 15 ml tbs olive oil
4 × 15 ml tbs white wine vinegar
1 × 15 ml tbs chopped fresh rosemary
25-50 g (1-2 oz) fresh Parmesan, crumbled or grated

1. Bat out the veal escalopes between sheets of greaseproof paper, then cut each into 4 strips.
2. Place a strip of ham on each piece of veal and roll up. Place in a non-metallic dish.

3. Mix together the oil, vinegar and rosemary and pour over the meat rolls. Marinate in the refrigerator for a few minutes (leave for several hours if you have the time).
4. Thread the veal and ham rolls on to skewers and reserve marinade.
5. Grill the kebabs under a moderate grill for about 12 minutes, turning frequently and basting with marinade. Sprinkle the cheese over each and grill for 1 minute, or until cheese just melts. Serve immediately.

LIVER AND BACON KEBABS

SERVES 4

450 g (1 lb) lamb's liver, trimmed and cut into large chunks
about 150 ml (5 fl oz) milk
225 g (8 oz) streaky bacon, rind removed
75 g (3 oz) butter or margarine
225-335g (8-12 oz) long-grain rice
salt and pepper
4 salad onions, finely chopped

1. Place the liver in a small bowl and cover with milk. Leave to soak in a cool place for 15–20 minutes.
2. Meanwhile, stretch each bacon rasher with the back of a knife, then cut in half and roll up.
3. Pat the liver dry on kitchen paper. Thread on to skewers with the bacon rolls. Brush with 25 g (1 oz) melted butter and cook under a preheated grill for 5–10 minutes, or until the liver is cooked through and the bacon is crisp.
4. Meanwhile, cook the rice in boiling salted water for about 8 minutes, or until tender.
5. Drain the rice. Place in a shallow serving dish and fork in the remaining butter with the salad onions. Top with the kebabs and serve.

Spiced Meatballs

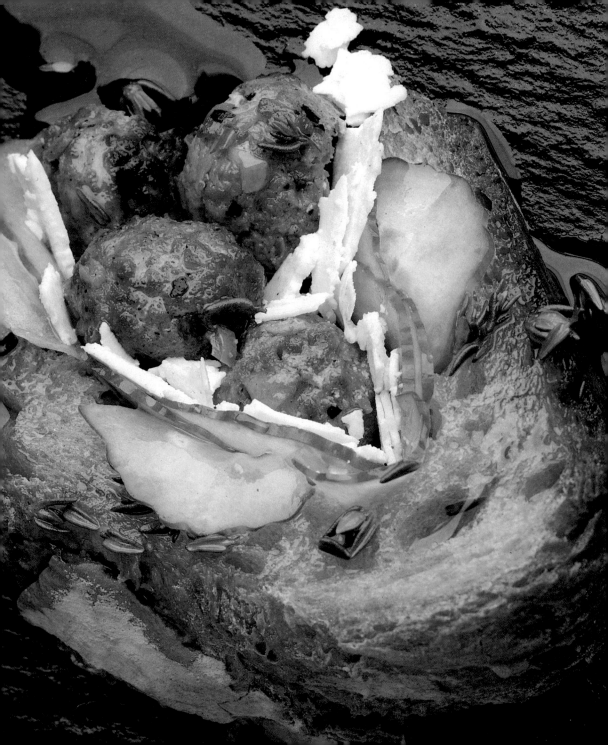

GOLDEN GRILLED SALMON

SERVES 4

3 × 15 ml tbs wholegrain mustard
2 × 15 ml tbs olive oil
1 × 5 ml tsp white wine vinegar
finely grated rind and juice of 1 lemon
salt and pepper
450 g (1 lb) salmon fillet, skinned and cut into
    2.5 cm (1 in) strips
150 ml (5 fl oz) milk
4 ×15 ml tbs double cream

1. To make the marinade, mix together the mustard, oil, vinegar, lemon rind and juice and seasoning in a large non-metallic bowl. Add the fish, cover and marinate in the refrigerator for 20 minutes.
2. Drain the salmon from the marinade and reserve the marinade. Grill fish on each side for 3-4 minutes, or until tender and golden brown. The fish will flake easily when it is cooked through.
3. Meanwhile, whisk the milk and cream into the reserved marinade. Heat gently until the sauce thickens. Do not boil. Serve immediately.

VARIATION Substitute 450 g (1 lb) skinned firm white fish fillet for the salmon. This is good served with boiled new potatoes and fresh or frozen green beans.

GRILLED SEAFOOD WITH ROMESCO SAUCE

SERVES 4

1 large red pepper
1-2 small red chillies, halved and seeded
150 g (5 oz) blanched almonds, toasted
4 large garlic cloves, skinned and crushed
small handful of fresh parsley
about 6 × 15 ml tbs red wine vinegar
salt and pepper
150 ml (5 fl oz) olive oil
a selection of fresh seafood, such as jumbo prawns,
    and firm white fish fillets
lemon wedges, to garnish

1. Place the pepper under the grill and cook, turning occasionally, until the skin chars and blackens. Cool under running water, then pull off the skin. Halve the pepper, discard the seeds and add the flesh to the bowl of a food processor.
2. Add the chillies to the food processor with the nuts, garlic, parsley, red wine vinegar and seasoning. Blend until almost smooth.
3. Slowly add the oil to the processor, pouring it through the feeder tube, as if making mayonnaise. The sauce should be thick and almost smooth. Adjust the seasoning, adding a little extra vinegar if wished.
4. Meanwhile, grill or barbecue a selection of mixed seafood until cooked through and the fish flesh flakes easily. Garnish with lemon wedges and serve with the sauce.

COOK'S TIPS A festival associated with the making of Romesco Sauce is held in Catalonia every year. You can also serve this robust sauce with grilled vegetables and meat, although it is exceptionally good with grilled seafood.
    The sauce can be covered and refrigerated for up to 1 week. Remove the sauce from the refrigerator 2 hours before you plan to serve it.

Spicy Chicken

SERVES 4

1 small green chilli, halved, seeded and finely chopped
about 4 × 15 ml tbs chopped fresh coriander or parsley
75g (3 oz) butter, softened
salt and pepper
4 chicken breast fillets with skin, about 150g (5 oz) each
2 × 15 ml tbs lemon juice
675 g (1½ lb) pumpkin or squash, peeled and cut into bite-sized pieces
225 g (8 oz) trimmed French beans, halved
fresh coriander sprigs, to garnish

1. Beat the chilli and coriander into the butter with seasoning.

2. Slash each side of the chicken three or four times to a depth of about 0.6 mm (¼ in) and place, skin side down, on a grill pan. Spread with half the butter and sprinkle with lemon juice.

3. Grill under a moderate heat for 7 minutes, then turn and spread with remaining butter. Grill for a further 7 minutes. Reserve any melted butter.

4. Meanwhile, cook the pumpkin and beans in boiling salted water for 5–10 minutes or until just tender; drain.

5. Serve the chicken with the vegetables, spooning over any reserved butter. Garnish with coriander.

Spicy Chicken

STIR-FRIES AND SAUTÉS

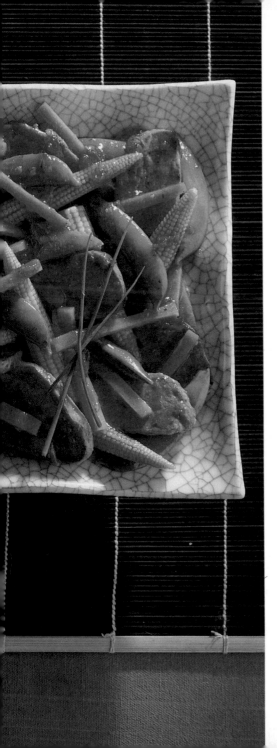

HOT AND SOUR PORK

SERVES 4

175 g (6 oz) onion, skinned and roughly chopped
3 garlic cloves, skinned and halved
2.5 cm (1 in) piece fresh root ginger, peeled
2 large red chillies, seeded
25 g (1 oz) blanched almonds, chopped
6 × 15 ml tbs olive oil
675 g (1½ lb) lean pork tenderloin, cut into 2.5 cm
 (1 in) cubes
3 × 15 ml tbs distilled malt vinegar
4 × 5 ml tsp caster sugar
2 × 15 ml tbs lemon juice
227 g can bamboo shoots, drained
2 × 15 ml tbs chopped fresh mint
salt and pepper

1. Place onion, garlic, ginger, chillies, almonds and 4 × 15 ml tbs of the oil in a food processor and blend until smooth.
2. Heat 2 × 15 ml tbs of the oil in a wok or large frying pan and stir-fry the pork in batches for 7–8 minutes. Remove with a slotted spoon and drain on kitchen paper.
3. Add chilli purée to the pan and stir-fry for about 2 minutes. Add the vinegar, sugar, lemon juice, 2 × 15 ml tbs water, pork and the bamboo shoots. Simmer for 2 minutes. Stir in the mint and season. Serve immediately with noodles.

VARIATION Substitute 675 g (1½ lb) skinless chicken breast fillets for the pork, cashew nuts for the almonds and chopped fresh coriander or parsley for the mint.

Hot and Sour Pork (left)
Stir-Fried Pork (right)

FRENCH-STYLE SAUSAGES WITH LENTILS

SERVES 4

2 × 15 ml tbs oil
450 g (1 lb) good-quality chunky sausages, skinned
  and sliced
6 large garlic cloves, unskinned
335 g (12 oz) small brown or green lentils, rinsed,
  boiled rapidly for 10 minutes then drained
225 g (8 oz) parsnips, peeled and cut into large
  chunks
about 900 ml (30 fl oz) chicken or vegetable stock
salt and pepper
finely chopped salad onions, to garnish

1. Heat the oil in a medium saucepan, preferably non-stick, and fry the sausage and garlic for about 3-4 minutes until golden.
2. Add the lentils and parsnips to the saucepan with the stock. Season and bring to the boil, then cover and simmer for about 20 minutes, or until the lentils are tender and much of the liquid absorbed. Add a little more stock during cooking, if necessary. Adjust the seasoning and serve garnished with the salad onions.

STIR-FRIED PORK

SERVES 4

175 g (6 oz) baby sweetcorn, drained if canned
175 g (6 oz) sugar-snap peas, topped and tailed
175 g (6 oz) carrot, peeled and cut into
  matchsticks
salt and pepper
3 × 15 ml tbs sunflower oil
450 g (1 lb) pork tenderloin, trimmed and cut into
  0.6 cm (¼ in) slices
4 × 15 ml tbs stir-fry chilli and tomato sauce
1 × 5 ml tsp caster sugar

2 × 15 ml tbs wine vinegar
4 × 15 ml tbs light soy sauce
fresh chives or sprigs of fresh parsley, to garnish

1. Blanch the baby sweetcorn, sugar-snap peas and carrots in boiling salted water for 2 minutes. Drain and refresh under cold running water.
2. Heat the oil in a larg wok or frying pan, preferably non-stick, and stir-fry the pork over a high heat for 2-3 minutes, or until well browned and almost tender.
3. Add the vegetables and continue stir-frying over a high heat for 2-3 minutes until piping hot.
4. Mix in the remaining ingredients and bring to the boil, stirring well. Adjust the seasoning and serve, garnished with chives or sprigs of parsley.

VARIATION Substitute 450 g (1 lb) lean rump steak for the pork tenderloin. Add 1 cored, seeded and thinly-sliced red pepper to the vegetables and proceed with the recipe.

CHEAT'S CASSOULET

SERVES 6

3 × 15 ml tbs oil
225 g (8 oz) onion, skinned and sliced
1 × 5 ml tsp ground paprika
225 g (8 oz) traditional German sausage, skinned
  and cut into chunks
200 g (7 oz) German salami, skinned and cut into
  chunks
1 garlic clove, skinned and crushed
2 × 5 ml tsp dried marjoram
150 ml (5 fl oz) chicken stock
1 × 15 ml tbs dry sherry
salt and pepper
2 × 450 g cans baked beans in tomato sauce
½ × 430 g can chick-peas, drained and rinsed

French-Style Sausages with Lentils

1. Heat the oil in a heavy-based saucepan and fry the onion until starting to brown and soften.
2. Mix in the paprika along with the meats. Stir over the heat for 2-3 minutes to blend in the paprika thoroughly, then stir in the garlic, marjoram, stock, sherry, seasoning and baked beans and chick-peas.
3. Bring slowly to the boil, stirring frequently, then cover and simmer for about 5 minutes or until really hot. Adjust the seasoning and serve immediately.

COOK'S TIP Traditional cassoulet is made from beans soaked and then simmered for hours. This cheat's version makes a delicious alternative to the time-honoured method.

57

ONE-POT LAMB

SERVES 4

3 × 15 ml tbs oil
8 lamb cutlets, about 675 g (1½ lb) total weight,
 well trimmed
450 g (1 lb) potatoes, peeled and cut into
 1 cm (½ in) cubes
225 g (8 oz) onion, skinned and roughly chopped
2 × 5 ml tsp chopped fresh rosemary or
 1 × 5 ml tsp dried
finely grated rind of 2 lemons
4 × 15 ml tbs lemon juice
150 ml (5 fl oz) beef stock
salt and pepper

1. Heat 2 × 15 ml tbs of the oil in a small
flameproof casserole and brown the cutlets well
on both sides, a few at a time. Remove with a
slotted spoon and drain well on absorbent
kitchen paper.
2. Add the remaining oil, potatoes and onion,
and stir over a high heat until beginning to
brown. Remove from the heat and stir in the
rosemary, lemon rind, lemon juice and the
stock. Return the lamb to the casserole.
3. Bring to the boil, then cover and simmer for
about 15 minutes or until the lamb and
potatoes are tender. Adjust the seasoning.

SPICED COCONUT LAMB

SERVES 4

115 g (4 oz) onion, skinned and roughly chopped
1 red chilli, seeded
2 × 15 ml tbs oil
2 garlic cloves, skinned
25 g (1 oz) blanched almonds
½ × 5 ml tsp ground turmeric
½ × 5 ml tsp ground ginger
8 lean lamb cutlets, about 450 g (1 lb) total weight
juice of 1 lemon
grated rind of 1 lemon
1 × 5 ml tsp dark muscovado sugar
225 ml (8 fl oz) thick coconut milk
salt and pepper
fresh coriander sprigs, to garnish

1. Place the onion, chilli, oil, garlic, nuts and
spices in a blender or food processor and blend
to a paste.
2. Fry the paste in a wok or large frying pan,
stirring constantly, for 1-2 minutes. Add the
lamb cutlets and cook over a medium heat,
until well browned on both sides.
3. Stir in the lemon juice, lemon rind,
muscovado sugar, coconut milk and 150 ml
(5 fl oz) water. Bring to the boil, then cover
and simmer gently for about 15 minutes, or
until the cutlets are tender.
4. Uncover and bubble down the juices for 3-4
minutes, to give a coating consistency, stirring
occasionally to prevent the sauce from sticking
to the pan.
5. Adjust seasoning and serve garnished with
coriander sprigs.

COOK'S TIP To make 600 ml (20 fl oz) thin
coconut milk, put ½ × 200 g (7 oz) packet
creamed coconut in a heatproof measuring jug
and pour in boiling water to come up to the
600 ml (20 fl oz) mark. Stir until dissolved. For
thick milk, use the whole packet.

Spiced Coconut Lamb

VENISON STEAK WITH POMEGRANATE

SERVES 4–6

2 pomegranates
675 g (1½ lb) venison steaks
salt and freshly ground pepper
2 × 15 ml tbs plain flour
6 × 15 ml tbs vegetable oil
115 g (4 oz) mushrooms, wiped and thickly sliced
400 ml (14 fl oz) chicken stock

1. Using a sharp knife, halve the pomegranates.

Scoop out and reserve the seeds and juices. Discard the membrane.

2. Divide each venison steak into two or three pieces. Place between sheets of damp greaseproof paper and bat out until the venison steak is quite thin. Season the flour and use to coat the meat pieces, shaking off and reserving any excess.

3. Heat the oil in a large sauté or frying pan and brown the venison, a quarter at a time. Return all the meat to the pan with any remaining flour. Add the mushrooms and stock with the pomegranate seeds and juices.

4. Bring to the boil and simmer for 2-3 minutes or until thoroughly hot. Adjust the seasoning before serving.

59

SAUTÉED LIVER WITH ORANGE AND SAGE

SERVES 4

450 g (1 lb) lamb's liver, cut into 5 cm (2 in) strips
25 g (1 oz) seasoned flour
2 × 5 ml tsp chopped fresh sage
3 large oranges
1 × 15 ml tbs oil
225 g (8 oz) onions, roughly chopped
chopped fresh sage or parsley, to garnish

1. Toss the liver in the seasoned flour and sage mixed together. Using a serrated knife, peel, halve and thickly slice one orange.
2. Heat the oil in a frying pan, add the onions and cook, stirring, for about 3-4 minutes. Add the liver and toss over a high heat for a further 5-7 minutes until browned and just cooked.
3. Reduce the heat, stir in the grated rind and juice of the remaining 2 oranges and allow to heat through. Garnish with the orange slices and sage or parsley and serve with pasta.

SAUTÉED LIVER WITH SAGE AND APPLE

SERVES 4

450 g (1 lb) calf's liver, trimmed and thinly sliced
25 g (1 oz) plain flour
3 × 15 ml tbs oil
115 g (4 oz) leeks, trimmed, sliced, and rinsed
1 × 5 ml tsp dried sage or dried mixed herbs
1 × 15 ml tbs mustard, preferably wholegrain
150 ml (5 fl oz) single cream
300 ml (10 fl oz) apple juice
salt and pepper

1. Cut the liver into small slices. Sprinkle the flour on to a flat plate and coat the liver.

2. Heat 2 × 15 ml tbs of the oil in a large sauté pan, (preferably non-stick), and brown the liver well for about 30 seconds on each side. Remove with a slotted spoon.
3. Add the remaining oil, the leeks and sage to the pan. Sauté, stirring well, for 2-3 minutes, then mix in the mustard, cream and apple juice. Bring to the boil and bubble for about 5 minutes, or until sauce is reduced by half.
4. Return the liver, season and simmer very gently for 1-2 minutes until heated through.

STIR-FRIED LIVER WITH CABBAGE AND CARAWAY

SERVES 4

15 g (½ oz) butter
1 × 15 ml tbs vegetable oil
450 g (1 lb) lamb's liver, trimmed and cut into 5 cm (2 in) strips
335 g (12 oz) green cabbage, finely shredded
1 large onion, skinned and chopped
1 Discovery or Crispin apple, quartered, cored and thinly sliced
1 × 15 ml tbs caraway seeds
2 × 15 ml tbs cider vinegar
1 × 15 ml tbs light demerara sugar

1. Heat the butter and oil in large frying pan and stir-fry the liver a few pieces at a time. Do not over-cook them, as the centres should be juicy. Remove with a slotted spoon.
2. Stir the cabbage and onion into the pan and stir-fry over a high heat for 4-5 minutes until the vegetables begin to soften.
3. Add the apple, caraway seeds, vinegar and sugar. Continue to stir-fry over a moderate heat for 1-2 minutes. Return the liver to the pan, season and re-heat very quickly. Serve.

Sautéed Liver with Orange and Sage

STRIPS OF BEEF IN WHISKY SAUCE

SERVES 6

15 g (½ oz) butter
675 g (1½ lb) sirloin steak, cut into strips
I large onion, skinned and chopped
3 × 15 ml tbs whisky liqueur, such as Glayva
75 ml (3 fl oz) double cream
salt and pepper

1. Melt the butter in a medium frying pan and fry the beef strips and onion for 5–10 minutes until the beef is brown and cooked to taste.
2. Stir in the liqueur and cream. Heat gently to reduce slightly. Adjust the seasoning and serve immediately with boiled rice and vegetables.

DRY-FRIED SWEET SPICED BEEF

SERVES 4

675 g (1½ lb) rump steak, cut into wafer-thin, bite-sized pieces
4 cm (1½ in) piece fresh root ginger, peeled and finely chopped
¾ × 5 ml tsp Tabasco sauce
¾ × 5 ml tsp ground cumin
2 × 5 ml tsp dark muscovado sugar
3 × 15 ml tbs oil
175 g (6 oz) onion, skinned and thinly sliced
3 × 15 ml tbs lemon juice
75 ml (3 fl oz) beef stock
salt and pepper
fresh chives, to garnish

1. Mix together the beef, ginger, Tabasco sauce, cumin and sugar. Cover and leave to marinate for at least 15 minutes (leave for longer if you have the time).

2. Heat the oil in a wok or or a frying pan and stir-fry the onion until golden brown. Add beef mixture and stir-fry until just browned and tender, 4–5 minutes.
3. Add lemon juice and stock. Bring to the boil and bubble until all the excess liquid has evaporated. Adjust the seasoning, garnish with chives and serve immediately with noodles.

CHICKEN AND GINGER STIR-FRY

SERVES 4

I × 5 ml tsp cornflour
2 × 15 ml tbs vinegar
2 × 15 ml tbs soy sauce
I × 15 ml tbs honey
salt and pepper
2 × 15 ml tbs oil
335 g (12 oz) chicken breast fillets, skinned and cut into very thin strips
175 g (6 oz) carrots, very thinly sliced
25 g (1 oz) piece fresh root ginger, peeled and finely chopped
I bunch salad onions, each cut into 3 or 4 pieces
I green or yellow pepper, seeded and finely shredded
175 g (6 oz) fresh beansprouts, rinsed

1. Mix the cornflour with 4 × 15 ml tbs water to form a smooth paste. Stir in the vinegar, soy sauce, honey and seasoning.
2. Heat the oil in a wok or large frying pan, and stir-fry the chicken, carrots and ginger over a high heat for 2–3 minutes, or until browned.
3. Stir in the onions, pepper and beansprouts and stir-fry for 2–3 minutes, until just tender.
4. Blend in the soy mixture then bring to the boil, stirring. Bubble for 1–2 minutes. Adjust seasoning and serve immediately.

Strips of Beef in Whisky Sauce

TURKEY SAUTÉ WITH LEMON AND WALNUTS

SERVES 4

450 g (1 lb) turkey breast fillets, skinned and cut
 into 5 cm (2 in) thin strips
2 × 15 ml tbs cornflour
2 × 15 ml tbs vegetable oil
1 green pepper, seeded and thinly sliced
40 g (1½ oz) walnut halves
25 g (1 oz) butter or margarine
4 × 15 ml tbs chicken stock
2 × 15 ml tbs lemon juice
3 × 15 ml tbs lemon marmalade
1 × 5 ml tsp white wine vinegar
¼ × 5 ml tsp soy sauce
salt and pepper

1. Toss the turkey strips in the cornflour until
coated.
2. Heat the oil in a large sauté or deep frying
pan and fry the pepper strips and walnuts for
2-3 minutes. Remove from the pan with a
slotted spoon and set aside.
3. Add the butter or margarine to the oil
remaining in the pan and fry the turkey strips
for 10 minutes, or until golden. Add the stock
and lemon juice, stirring well to scrape up any
sediment at the bottom of the pan. Add the
lemon marmalade, vinegar and soy sauce.
Season to taste.
4. Return the walnuts and green pepper to the
pan. Cook gently for a further 5 minutes, or
until the turkey is tender. Taste and adjust the
seasoning and serve immediately.

VARIATION Substitute 2 × 15 ml tbs orange
juice and 3 × 15 ml tbs orange marmalade for
the lemon juice and marmalade in the recipe.
Garnish with thin slices or wedges of orange.

Turkey Sauté with Lemon and Walnuts

STIR-FRIED DUCKLING WITH MANGETOUT

SERVES 4

150 ml (5 fl oz) chicken stock
2 × 15 ml tbs soy sauce
1 × 15 ml tbs cornflour
1 × 5 ml tsp light muscovado sugar
335 g (12 oz) duckling breast fillets, skinned and
 cut into thin strips
1 × 15 ml tbs hoisin sauce
1 × 15 ml tbs dry sherry
2 × 15 ml tbs oil
1 garlic clove, skinned and crushed
2.5 cm (1 in) piece of fresh root ginger, peeled
 and chopped
1 bunch of salad onions, trimmed and cut into
 2.5 cm (1 in) lengths
230 g can whole water chestnuts, drained and
 thinly sliced
225 g (8 oz) mangetout, topped and tailed
salt and pepper

1. Mix together the stock, soy sauce, half the
cornflour and the sugar. Mix the duckling with
remaining cornflour, hoisin sauce and sherry.
2. Heat 1 × 15 ml tbs of the oil in a wok or
heavy-based frying pan and fry the garlic and
ginger for about 5 minutes, or until soft. Turn
up the heat. Add the duckling and stir-fry until
the meat changes colour. Remove from the
pan with a slotted spoon and set aside.
3. Heat the remaining oil in the pan and stir-fry
the salad onions for 1 minute. Add the water
chestnuts and mangetout and stir-fry for
another minute.
4. Add the duckling and stock mixture and
cook, stirring continually, until bubbling.
Season to taste and serve immediately.

COOK'S TIP Removing the skin from duck
dramatically reduces the fat content; duck flesh
contains no more fat than chicken flesh.

Smoked Mackerel and Cucumber Stir-Fry

SERVES 2

2 × 5 ml tsp sesame seeds
1 × 15 ml tbs oil
½ cucumber cut into 5 cm (2 in) long thick strips
1 bunch of salad onions, shredded
175 g (6 oz) peppered smoked mackerel fillets, skinned and cut, into 2.5 cm (1 in) strips
1 × 15 ml tbs soy sauce
2 × 5 ml tsp lemon juice

1. Toast the sesame seeds under the grill, watching them carefully so they do not burn. Set aside.
2. Heat the oil in a wok or large frying pan and stir-fry the cucumber and salad onions over a high heat for 2-3 minutes until softened.
3. Mix in the fish and stir-fry carefully for a further minute before adding the soy sauce and lemon juice. Allow to bubble up, sprinkle over the sesame seeds and serve immediately.

Light Seafood Stir-Fry

SERVES 4

2 × 15 ml tbs oil
450 g (1 lb) firm white fish fillet, skinned and cut into bite-sized pieces
1 bunch of salad onions, sliced
1 garlic clove, skinned and finely chopped
2.5 cm (1 in) piece fresh root ginger, peeled and finely chopped
275 g (10 oz) leeks, trimmed, sliced, rinsed and drained
1 red pepper, seeded and roughly chopped
115 g (4 oz) peeled cooked prawns
1 × 15 ml tbs each hoisin sauce, light soy sauce and dry sherry
black pepper

1. Heat the oil in a large non-stick wok or frying pan and stir-fry the fish for 2-3 minutes. Remove with a slotted spoon and set aside.
2. Stir-fry the onions, garlic and ginger for 2 minutes, or until beginning to soften. Add the leeks and pepper and stir-fry for a further 10 minutes until softened.
3. Return the fish to the pan with the prawns, hoisin sauce, soy sauce and sherry. Season with plenty of black pepper (the soy sauce is fairly salty). Cook for 1 minute, stirring. Serve.

Spiced Fish Stir-Fry

SERVES 4

1 × 5 ml tsp plain flour
2 × 5 ml tsp ground coriander
2 × 5 ml tsp ground cumin
450 g (1 lb) haddock fillet, skinned and cut into strips
3 × 15 ml tbs oil
1 small green pepper, seeded and thinly sliced
1 small yellow pepper, seeded and thinly sliced
1 medium onion, skinned and thinly sliced
225 g (8 oz) tomatoes, skinned and chopped
115 g (4 oz) fresh beansprouts, rinsed
5 × 15 ml tbs dry white wine
chopped fresh coriander or parsley
salt and pepper

1. Mix the flour and spices together on a plate and use to coat the fish.
2. Heat a little oil in 2 woks or frying pans. Add the peppers and onion to one pan and stir-fry over a high heat until beginning to brown.
3. Add the fish to the other wok or frying pan and stir-fry for 2-3 minutes.
4. Add the tomatoes and beansprouts to the vegetables and cook for 2-3 minutes or until the tomatoes begin to soften.
5. Stir the contents of both pans together. Mix in the wine with a little fresh coriander and seasoning and bubble up. Serve immediately.

Piquant Haddock

SERVES 4

675 g (1½ lb) fresh haddock fillet, skinned and cut into bite-sized pieces
1½ × 5 ml tsp each ground cumin and coriander
½ × 5 ml tsp each ground turmeric and ginger
salt and pepper
300 ml (10 fl oz) natural yogurt
2 × 15 ml tbs lemon juice
1 × 15 ml tbs vegetable oil
225 g (8 oz) onion, skinned and chopped
2 × 15 ml tbs plain flour
150 ml (5 fl oz) fish stock
chopped fresh parsley, to garnish

1. Mix the haddock with the spices, seasoning, yogurt and lemon juice. Cover and marinate for a few minutes (or overnight if you have the time) in the refrigerator.
2. Heat the oil in a large saucepan and sauté the onion for 6–7 minutes, or until beginning to soften. Off the heat, stir in the flour, then blend in the stock. Carefully stir in the fish and yogurt mixture.
3. Bring to the boil, stirring, then cover and simmer very gently for 5 minutes or until tender. Garnish with chopped fresh parsley. Serve immediately.

Piquant Haddock

CAPPUCCINO CREAMS

SERVES 8

500 g fromage frais
2 × 15 ml tbs finely-ground espresso coffee
2 × 15 ml tbs icing sugar (optional)
175 g (6 oz) dark or bitter chocolate
chocolate curls, to decorate

1. Mix the fromage frais with the coffee and icing sugar, if using.
2. Pulverise the chocolate in a blender until very fine, or grate finely.
3. Spoon half the fromage frais into eight ramekins or glass dishes. Sprinkle over most of the chocolate mixture. Top with the remaining fromage frais and sprinkle with the remaining chocolate mixture to give a speckled appearance like cappuccino. Decorate with chocolate curls.

LEMON BRULÉE

SERVES 4

finely grated rind of 1 lemon
450 g (1 lb) Greek-style yogurt
2 × 15 ml tbs soft dark brown sugar

1. Mix together the lemon rind and the yogurt. Divide between four 150 ml (5 fl oz) ramekins and sprinkle the sugar over the top.
2. Place under a hot grill for 1–2 minutes or until melted and bubbling.
3. Chill until ready to serve.

VARIATION Substitute the finely-grated rind of 2 limes for the lemon rind. This is delicious served with fresh strawberries.

Cappuccino Creams

FIGS WITH WARM BERRY SAUCE

SERVES 4

8 ripe figs, stalks removed
210 g can blackberries in apple juice
2 × 5 ml tsp icing sugar
1 × 5 ml tsp arrowroot
mint or lemon geranium leaves or borage flowers,
    to decorate

1. In each fig, make 2 cuts in a cross shape, from the stalk end, three-quarters of the way down. Open up to resemble a flower. Place 2 figs on each plate.
2. Push the blackberries and juice through a nylon sieve into a small saucepan. Add the icing sugar. Mix the arrowroot with a little water to form a smooth paste.
3. Gently heat the sauce until simmering. Remove from the heat and stir in the arrowroot. Return to the heat and boil for 1 minute, stirring.
4. Pour a little sauce over each fig. Decorate with mint or lemon geranium leaves or borage flowers, if wished. Serve the remaining sauce in a separate jug.

COOK'S TIP You could also serve this sauce with slices of galia melon or quartered fresh pears.

EXOTIC FRUIT SALAD

SERVES 4

900 g (2 lb) ripe pineapple
1 mango or small papaya
1 guava or banana, sliced
1 passion fruit or pomegranate
4 lychees or rambutans
1 kiwi fruit

1. Cut the pineapple in half lengthways, with the leaves attached, Remove the core in a wedge from each half and discard. Cut the flesh away from the skin, cut it into small chunks and place in a bowl. Scrape out any remaining flesh and juice with a spoon and add to bowl.
2. Peel the mango or papaya and remove the stone or seeds. Cut the flesh into cubes and add to the pineapple with the guava or banana.
3. Cut the passion fruit or pomegranate in half and scoop out the seeds with a teaspoon. Add the seeds to the pineapple.
4. Peel the lychees or rambutans and cut in half. Remove the stones and add to the bowl of fruit.
5. Peel the kiwi fruit and cut the flesh into round slices. Add to the bowl of fruit and stir.
6. Spoon the fruit salad into the pineapple halves. Cover and chill until required.

SUMMER CURRANT COMPOTE

SERVES 6

50-75 g (2-3 oz) granulated sugar
225 g (8 oz) blackcurrants, stalks removed
450 g (1 lb) redcurrants, stalks removed
pared rind and juice of 1 medium orange
2 × 15 ml tbs honey
335 (12 oz) strawberries, hulled and sliced

1. Dissolve the sugar in 150 ml (5 fl oz) water in a pan. Boil for 1 minute. Add the currants and orange rind and simmer until the fruits are just beginning to soften – about 1 minute only.
2. Carefully transfer the fruits and syrup to a serving bowl. Stir in the honey and orange juice, then add the strawberries. Serve at once.

VARIATION Add the honey, leave to cool, then stir in the orange juice. Cover and chill well. Just before serving, stir the strawberries into the compote.

Figs with Warm Berry Sauce

Hot Fruit Salad

SERVES 4

8 no-soak prunes
2 oranges
2 bananas, about 175 g (6 oz) each
25 g (1 oz) low-fat spread
2 × 15 ml tbs demerara sugar
150 ml (5 fl oz) fresh unsweetened orange juice

1. Stone and halve the prunes. Using a serrated knife, peel and segment the oranges. Peel and thickly slice the bananas.
2. Melt the fat in a medium, preferably non-stick, sauté pan. Add the sugar and prepared fruit. Toss together over a high heat for 1 minute before adding the orange juice. Bring to the boil, then remove from the heat. Serve hot.

Damson and Apple Tansy

SERVES 4

2 large Cox's apples, peeled, cored and thinly
    sliced
225 g (8 oz) damsons, halved, stoned and
    quartered
15 g (½ oz) butter
40 g (1½ oz) sugar
pinch of ground cloves
pinch of ground cinnamon
4 × size 3 eggs, separated
3 × 15 ml tbs soured cream

1. Put the apples, damsons, butter and half the sugar in a large frying pan. Cook over a gentle heat until the fruit is softened, stirring continuously. Stir in the cloves and cinnamon, then remove from the heat.
2. Beat the egg yolks and cream together and

stir into the fruit. Whisk the egg whites until stiff, then fold in.
3. Cook over a low heat until the eggs are cooked and the mixture has set. Sprinkle the top with the remaining sugar, then brown under a hot grill. Serve immediately, straight from the pan, with soured cream.

Sparkling Melon and Strawberries

SERVES 6

1 orange-fleshed charentais or cantaloupe melon,
    halved and seeded
1 green-fleshed ogen or galia melon, halved and
    seeded
225 g (8 oz) small strawberries, hulled
1 × 15 ml tbs icing sugar
1 × 15 ml tbs brandy
200 ml (7 fl oz) sparkling white wine or
    champagne, chilled
fresh mint leaves, to decorate

1. Use a melon baller to cut the melon flesh into balls.
2. Put fruits in a bowl with sugar and brandy. Cover and chill for 10–15 minutes.
3. Divide among bowls and pour over the sparkling wine or champagne. Decorate with mint leaves.

VARIATION For a non-alcoholic version, substitute sparkling apple juice for the sparkling wine.

Hot Fruit Salad

PEAR AND APRICOT CHARLOTTE

SERVES 4

410 g can apricot halves in natural juice,
  drained
415 g can pears halves in natural juice, drained
25 g (1 oz) split almonds
butter or margarine
6 thin slices of rich fruit loaf
a little demerara sugar
150 ml (5 fl oz) single cream
150 ml (5 fl oz) Greek-style yogurt

1. Purée the apricots and pour over the pears in an ovenproof serving dish. Sprinkle over the almonds.
2. Lightly butter the fruit loaf. Cut each slice into four triangles and arrange, butter-side up, overlapping over the fruit. Sprinkle with demerara sugar.
3. Bake in the oven at 190°C/375°F/Gas Mark 5 for 20-30 minutes or until crisp and golden. Serve hot accompanied with cream and yogurt mixed.

GRILLED FRUIT WITH SWEET GINGER BUTTER

SERVES 6-8

selection of tropical fruit, such as pineapple
  wedges, slices of pawpaw, mango chunks and
  banana halves
115 g (4 oz) unsalted butter
2 × 15 ml tbs finely chopped stem ginger, or
  peeled, fresh root ginger
2 × 5 ml tsp icing sugar
2 × 5 ml tsp lemon juice
natural yogurt or single cream, to serve

1. Prepare a selection of tropical fruit. Melt the butter and stir in the ginger, icing sugar and the lemon juice.
2. Place the fruit on the barbecue or under a hot grill. Brush lightly with the butter mixture and cook, turning and brushing with the butter, for 5-7 minutes, or until beginning to caramelise and blacken. Serve immediately with natural yogurt or single cream.

COOK'S TIP To prepare the mango, stand the fruit on its narrow edge and cut thick slices from either side of the stone. Score the flesh in a wide criss-cross pattern and push the skin up towards the flesh to expose the mango chunks.

APRICOT AND ORANGE CUSTARDS

SERVES 6

500 g natural fromage frais
450 ml (15 fl oz) fresh custard sauce
2 oranges
410 g can apricot halves in natural juice
caster sugar, to taste (optional)
sweet biscuits and single cream, to serve

1. Whisk together the fromage frais and the custard sauce until blended.
2. Finely grate the rind of the oranges and stir into the custard mixture with 4 × 15 ml tbs strained orange juice. Mix thoroughly.
3. Drain the apricots, place in a blender or food processor and process until quite smooth. Add caster sugar to taste.
4. Spoon the custard into six tall, stemmed glasses and top each with the apricot purée. Serve accompanied with sweet biscuits and single cream.

Grilled Fruit with Sweet Ginger Butter

PLUM AND NUT CRUMBLE

SERVES 4

2 × 560 g cans red plums in syrup, drained
ground cinnamon, to taste
115 g (4 oz) plain wholemeal flour
50 g (2 oz) butter or margarine, chilled
115 g (4 oz) soft dark brown sugar
50 g (2 oz) walnuts, chopped
25 g (1 oz) porridge oats
custard, to serve

1. Place the plums in a 1.5 lt (2½ pt) ovenproof serving dish. Sprinkle over ground cinnamon to taste.
2. Place the flour and butter in a food processor and blend briefly until the mixture looks like breadcrumbs. Stir in the sugar, walnuts and oats. Sprinkle over the plums, roughly levelling the surface.
3. Bake in the oven at 180°C/350°F/Gas Mark 4 for 20–30 minutes, or until golden. Serve hot or cold with custard.

FRUITED RICE PUDDING

SERVES 4

75 g (3 oz) pudding rice
25 g (1 oz) caster sugar
40 g (1½ oz) butter
900 ml (30 fl oz) milk
40 g (1½ oz) sultanas
40 g (1½ oz) candied peel, chopped
grated rind and juice of 1 lemon

1. Place all the ingredients, except lemon juice, in a medium saucepan. Bring to the boil, then simmer for 25–30 minutes, or until the rice is tender, stirring occasionally.
2. Take off the heat then mix in lemon juice to taste. Serve immediately.

APRICOT ORANGE CRISP

SERVES 4

grated rind and juice of ½ small orange
2 × 410 g cans apricot halves in natural juice, drained
75 g (3 oz) butter or margarine
175 g (6 oz) plain flour
50 g (2 oz) chopped blanched almonds
50 g (2 oz) demerara sugar

1. Stir the orange rind and juice into the fruit and warm in a pan. Spoon into a 1.2 lt (2 pt) ovenproof dish.
2. While the fruit is warming, rub the fat into the flour until the mixture resembles breadcrumbs. Stir in the almonds and sugar. Sprinkle over the apricots and grill lightly. Serve warm.

RHUBARB SPONGE MERINGUE

SERVES 4

4 trifle sponge cakes
525 g can rhubarb
finely grated rind of 1 orange
2 × 15 ml tbs orange juice
2 egg whites
50 g (2 oz) caster sugar

1. Place the sponge cakes in a 1.8 lt (3 pt) soufflé dish. Add the rhubarb with the rind and orange juice.
2. Whisk the egg whites until stiff. Mix in half the sugar and whisk again until stiff and shiny. Fold in the remaining sugar. Spoon roughly over the top of the rhubarb mixture.
3. Bake in the oven at 180°C/350°F/Gas Mark 4 for 10–15 minutes, until crisp and golden. Serve hot.

Apricot Orange Crisp

ORANGE AND NECTARINE CRÊPES

SERVES 4

115 g (4 oz) plain flour
pinch of salt
1 × size 3 egg
300 ml (10 fl oz) milk
vegetable oil for frying
grated rind and juice of 2 oranges
50 g (2 oz) caster sugar
4 large, ripe nectarines
2 × 15 ml tbs orange-flavoured liqueur
3 × 15 ml tbs brandy

1. Sift the flour and salt into a bowl and make a well in the centre. Break in the egg and beat well with a wooden spoon, then gradually beat in the milk, drawing in the flour from the sides to make a smooth batter.
2. Heat a little oil in an 18 cm (7 in) heavy-based frying pan. Pour in just enough batter to thinly coat the base of the pan. Cook for 1–2 minutes until golden brown, then turn and cook the second side. Repeat with the remaining batter to make eight crêpes. Stack the crêpes with greaseproof paper in between and keep warm in the oven.
3. Make the orange juice up to 150 ml (5 fl oz) with water. Place the rind and juice in a saucepan with the sugar. Warm gently until the sugar dissolves, then boil for 1 minute.
4. Meanwhile, quarter each nectarine, skin and roughly chop the flesh. Place the flesh in the syrup and simmer gently for 3–4 minutes. Remove from the heat and stir in the liqueur. Strain off the syrup and reserve.
5. Fill the crêpes with the nectarines, then fold each one into a fan shape. Place, slightly overlapping, in a greased ovenproof dish. Pour over the syrup and cover tightly with greased foil. Bake in the oven at 200°C/400°F/Gas Mark 6 for about 15 minutes or until hot.

6. Place the brandy in a small saucepan. Warm slightly, then set alight with a match and immediately pour over the crêpes. Serve with cream or yogurt.

VARIATION Divide 2 × 350 g jars chunky apple with no added sugar between the crêpes. Sprinkle with sugar, then fold over and arrange in the dish. Dot with 50 g (2 oz) unsalted butter, diced, then heat in the oven as before. Warm 3 × 15 ml tbs calvados in a saucepan. Set alight and pour over the crêpes.

BEIGNETS DE FRUITS

SERVES 4

115 g (4 oz) plain flour
pinch of salt
1 × 15 ml tbs icing sugar
1 egg
150 ml (5 fl oz) beer
oil for deep-frying
1 large eating apple, peeled, cored and cut into rings
1 firm nectarine, stoned and cut into quarters
1 banana, peeled and cut into chunks
caster sugar for sprinkling

1. Sift the flour, salt and icing sugar into a bowl and make a well in the centre. Break in the egg and beat well with a wooden spoon, then gradually beat in the beer, drawing in the flour from the sides to make a smooth batter.
2. Heat the oil in a deep-fryer to 190°C/375°F. Dip the prepared fruits in the batter and deep-fry in batches. The apple will take about 4 minutes and the nectarine and banana about 3 minutes.
3. Drain on absorbent kitchen paper and keep warm while frying the remainder. Serve hot sprinkled with caster sugar.

Beignets de Fruits

apricot and orange custards, 74
apricot orange crisp, 76
aubergine and bean gratin, 39
aubergine risotto, 37
avocado and chick-pea salad, 17

bacon sauce, pasta with, 32
beef: dry-fried, 62
  sirloin steaks with mustard, 49
  strips in whisky sauce, 62
beignets de fruits, 78
broccoli purée, 12

cappuccino creams, 69
cauliflower gratin, 40
cheat's cassoulet, 56–7
cheesy vegetable soup, 14
chick-peas: artichoke heart salad
  with, 20
  mushroom bake with, 44
chicken: glazed chicken rice
  casserole, 36
  spicy chicken, 53
  stir-fry with ginger and, 62
  30-minute artichoke bake with,
  44
chicory and carrot gratin, 41
chicory salad, grilled, 18
Chinese rice pot, 36
chorizo and feta pizza, 28
cod and crab gratin, 40

damson and apple tansy, 73
desserts, 68–78
duckling, stir-fried, 65

egg and bacon pilaff, 32

figs with warm berry sauce, 70
French beans: bean and tuna salad,
  22
  French bean soup, 10
French-style sausages with lentils,
  56
fruit: beignets de fruits, 78
  exotic fruit salad, 70
  grilled fruit, 74
  hot fruit salad, 73
  summer currant compote, 70

garlic croûton salad, 22
gratins, 39–41

haddock: corn chowder with, 9
  piquant haddock, 67
  smoky bean salad, 23
  spiced fish stir-fry, 66
'hot' red salad, 24

Italian-style kebabs, 50

lamb: chops with rosemary, 47
  with minted orange sauce, 48
  one-pot lamb, 58
  spiced coconut lamb, 58
  spiced meatballs, 50
leek and lentil pilaff, 32
lemon brulée, 69
lentils: chunky soup, 10
  lentil and coconut soup, 10
liver: bacon kebabs with, 50
  sautéed with orange, 60
  sautéed with sage, 60
  stir-fried with cabbage, 60
  warm livers with bitter leaves, 20

mackerel: smoked mackerel and
  cucumber stir-fry, 66
meatballs, spiced, 50
Mediterranean salad, 24
melon and strawberries, 73
muffin pizzas, quick, 27
mushrooms: cashew-stuffed, 45
  cheese and chive, 42
  Parmesan risotto with, 35
  pasta with sautéed, 30

orange and nectarine crêpes, 78

paella with peppers, 35
pasta dishes, 30–2
pear and apricot charlotte, 74
peasant salad, 22
peperami, pasta with, 30
pepper, roasted pizza, 28
pizzas, 27–8
plum and nut crumble, 76
pork: golden grilled, 48
  hot and sour, 55
  stir-fried, 56

rhubarb sponge meringue, 76
rice dishes, 35–7
rice pudding, fruited, 76
Romesco sauce, 52

salads, 16–24
salami and cheese pizza, 27
salmon: golden grilled, 52
  warm salad, 20
sausages, French-style, 56
seafood: light stir-fry, 66
  Romesco sauce with, 52
smoky bean salad, 23
soups, 8–14
spicy bean and courgette soup, 12
summer platter, 18

tomato soup with bacon, 14
tuna and bean salad, 22
turkey sauté, 65

veal: Italian-style kebabs, 50
vegetables: cheesy soup, 14
  creamy vegetable pasta, 30
  cheese croûtes with, 42
venison with pomegranate, 59
vinaigrette dressing, 18

warm salad with bacon, 19
white bean and basil soup, 12